# Apress Pocket Guides

*Apress Pocket Guides* present concise summaries of cutting-edge developments and working practices throughout the tech industry. Shorter in length, books in this series aims to deliver quick-to-read guides that are easy to absorb, perfect for the time-poor professional.

This series covers the full spectrum of topics relevant to the modern industry, from security, AI, machine learning, cloud computing, web development, product design, to programming techniques and business topics too.

Typical topics might include:

- A concise guide to a particular topic, method, function or framework

- Professional best practices and industry trends

- A snapshot of a hot or emerging topic

- Industry case studies

- Concise presentations of core concepts suited for students and those interested in entering the tech industry

- Short reference guides outlining 'need-to-know' concepts and practices.

More information about this series at https://link.springer.com/bookseries/17385.

# Delegates, Events, and Lambda Expressions in C#

## A Hands-On Guide with Examples, Q&A, and Exercises

**Vaskaran Sarcar**

Apress®

*Delegates, Events, and Lambda Expressions in C#: A Hands-On Guide with Examples, Q&A, and Exercises*

Vaskaran Sarcar
Kolkata, West Bengal, India

ISBN-13 (pbk): 979-8-8688-2092-2             ISBN-13 (electronic): 979-8-8688-2093-9
https://doi.org/10.1007/979-8-8688-2093-9

## Copyright © 2025 by Vaskaran Sarcar

This work is subject to copyright. All rights are reserved by the Publisher, whether the whole or part of the material is concerned, specifically the rights of translation, reprinting, reuse of illustrations, recitation, broadcasting, reproduction on microfilms or in any other physical way, and transmission or information storage and retrieval, electronic adaptation, computer software, or by similar or dissimilar methodology now known or hereafter developed.

Trademarked names, logos, and images may appear in this book. Rather than use a trademark symbol with every occurrence of a trademarked name, logo, or image we use the names, logos, and images only in an editorial fashion and to the benefit of the trademark owner, with no intention of infringement of the trademark.

The use in this publication of trade names, trademarks, service marks, and similar terms, even if they are not identified as such, is not to be taken as an expression of opinion as to whether or not they are subject to proprietary rights.

While the advice and information in this book are believed to be true and accurate at the date of publication, neither the authors nor the editors nor the publisher can accept any legal responsibility for any errors or omissions that may be made. The publisher makes no warranty, express or implied, with respect to the material contained herein.

    Managing Director, Apress Media LLC: Welmoed Spahr
    Acquisitions Editor: Smriti Srivastava
    Coordinating Editor: Jessica Vakili

Cover designed by eStudioCalamar

Distributed to the book trade worldwide by Springer Science+Business Media New York, 1 New York Plaza, New York, NY 10004. Phone 1-800-SPRINGER, fax (201) 348-4505, e-mail orders-ny@springer-sbm.com, or visit www.springeronline.com. Apress Media, LLC is a Delaware LLC and the sole member (owner) is Springer Science + Business Media Finance Inc (SSBM Finance Inc). SSBM Finance Inc is a **Delaware** corporation.

For information on translations, please e-mail booktranslations@springernature.com; for reprint, paperback, or audio rights, please e-mail bookpermissions@springernature.com.

Apress titles may be purchased in bulk for academic, corporate, or promotional use. eBook versions and licenses are also available for most titles. For more information, reference our Print and eBook Bulk Sales web page at http://www.apress.com/bulk-sales.

Any source code or other supplementary material referenced by the author in this book is available to readers on GitHub (https://github.com/Apress/Delegates-Events-and-Lambda-Expressions-in-C). For more detailed information, please visit https://www.apress.com/gp/services/source-code.

If disposing of this product, please recycle the paper

*To those, seen or unseen, whose presence carried me through challenges and nurtured my growth.*

# Table of Contents

**About the Author** .................................................................xi

**About the Technical Reviewer** ...........................................xiii

**Acknowledgments** ............................................................xv

**Introduction** ....................................................................xvii

**Chapter 1: Delegates** ..........................................................1

Concept .......................................................................................1

Custom Delegates .......................................................................2

    Defining a Delegate ..............................................................2

    Assigning the Delegate Variable ............................................3

    Invoking the Delegate ...........................................................4

Multicasting ..............................................................................10

    Working on Invocation List ..................................................10

    Alternative Code .................................................................12

Built-In Delegates .....................................................................13

    Func Delegate ....................................................................14

    Action Delegate .................................................................15

Anonymous Method ..................................................................21

    Working on Anonymous Methods .......................................21

Useful Notes .............................................................................23

    You Worked with a Sealed Class ........................................24

    You Used a Shorthand Code ...............................................25

Summary ..................................................................................27

# TABLE OF CONTENTS

Exercise 1 .................................................................................. 28
    Keys to Exercise 1 ............................................................... 32

## Chapter 2: Events ................................................................. 37
Concept ...................................................................................... 37
    Designing a Publisher-Subscriber Model ........................... 38
Standard Event Guidelines ....................................................... 44
    First Update ........................................................................... 45
    Second Update ..................................................................... 46
    Third Update ......................................................................... 49
    Final Update ......................................................................... 53
Chaining Events ........................................................................ 55
    Adding More Handlers ......................................................... 55
Useful Notes ............................................................................. 59
    Be Careful Before Using the Anonymous Method ............ 59
    Event Modifiers .................................................................... 61
Summary ................................................................................... 61
Exercise 2 .................................................................................. 62
    Keys to Exercise 2 ............................................................... 64

## Chapter 3: Lambda Expressions ......................................... 69
Concept ...................................................................................... 69
    Programming Lambda Expressions .................................... 70
Types of Lambdas .................................................................... 74
    Executing Different Lambdas .............................................. 75
Uses of Lambda Expressions .................................................. 76
    Event Subscription ............................................................... 77
    Replacing the Anonymous Method .................................... 79

| | |
|---|---|
| Parallel Programming | 80 |
| Functional Programming | 81 |
| Useful Notes | 83 |
| Multiple Usages of the Token => | 83 |
| How Does the C# Compiler Transform the Lambdas? | 84 |
| Latest Feature | 85 |
| Further Reading | 87 |
| Summary | 88 |
| Exercise 3 | 88 |
| Keys to Exercise 3 | 89 |

## Chapter 4: Bonus ............................................................................93

| | |
|---|---|
| More on Delegates | 93 |
| Covariance | 93 |
| Contravariance | 96 |
| More on Events | 101 |
| Event Accessors | 101 |
| Interface Events | 106 |
| Events in a GUI App | 111 |
| Summary | 116 |
| Exercise 4 | 116 |
| Keys to Exercise 4 | 118 |

## Appendix A: What's Next? ...........................................................123

## Appendix B: Author's Other Books ...........................................125

# About the Author

**Vaskaran Sarcar**, a National GATE Scholar with dual master's degrees in Engineering and Computer Applications, has journeyed from lecturing in engineering colleges to leading teams at HP India's R&D hub. Author of 18 Apress books, he now channels his passion into writing, turning complex ideas into accessible knowledge to inspire learners worldwide. You can find his work at Amazon[1] and Springer.[2] You can connect with him on LinkedIn.[3]

---

[1] https://www.amazon.com/author/vaskaran_sarcar
[2] https://link.springer.com/search?newsearch=true&query=vaskaran+sarcar&content-type=book&dateFrom=&dateTo=&sortBy=newestFirst
[3] https://www.linkedin.com/in/vaskaransarcar

# About the Technical Reviewer

**Naga Santhosh Reddy Vootukuri** works for Microsoft as a principal software engineering manager in the Azure SQL product. He has more than 17 years of experience in designing and developing several products within Microsoft, ranging from SSIS to MDS, and currently in Azure SQL DB. He has deep knowledge in cloud computing, distributed systems, artificial intelligence, microservices-based architecture, and cloud-native apps and has experience working in three different Microsoft centers (India, China, and the United States).

At Microsoft, Naga leads the Azure SQL Database team, focusing on optimizing SQL deployment processes to enhance the efficiency and scalability of services for millions of databases globally. He is responsible for the entire infrastructure of the Azure SQL deployment space and has been instrumental in the development of SSIS and Master Data Services.

Santhosh has authored and published numerous research articles in peer-reviewed and indexed journals and in major trade publications. He is a core MVB blogger at DZone and an active senior IEEE member handling various conferences as technical chair in the Seattle IEEE region. He recently served as IEEE AI Summit Committee chair and lightning talk chair and selected some of the best lightning talks. He also delivered AI-related workshops and received an **AI innovator award from Washington Senator Lisa Wellman**.

## ABOUT THE TECHNICAL REVIEWER

Naga served as a judge for the Agent AI hackathon, Fabric AI hackathon, and Cosmos DB AI hackathon on DevPost, which further showcased his expertise and commitment to the advancement of technology. He also manages several open source projects on GitHub, which have several stars. He frequently speaks and presents at various conferences about microservices, AI, and cloud computing. He actively mentors junior engineers on ADPList and contributes widely to the developer community. Naga is in the top few developers list in the cloud and AI community. Naga has been awarded the prestigious Docker Captain membership program for his outstanding contributions to the Docker and containers community. You can connect with him on LinkedIn.

# Acknowledgments

First and foremost, I express my heartfelt gratitude to the Almighty. I firmly believe that it is by His blessings that I was able to complete this book.

My sincere thanks to **Naga Santhosh Reddy Vootukuri**, the technical reviewer for this book, and also for one of my earlier works. Your unwavering support, whether over phone calls, WhatsApp, or emails, has been invaluable. I truly appreciate your time, patience, and guidance.

To **Smriti, Jessica, Celestin,** and the entire **Apress team**—thank you for once again allowing me to collaborate with you. It's always a pleasure working together.

To **Nirmal, the Copy Editor Rohini Kannan,** and the **Production team members Vinoth and Nagarajan**—your exceptional effort in refining and enhancing my work has been extraordinary. I deeply appreciate the care and dedication you bring to every detail.

Finally, I extend my gratitude to members of various online communities—especially the C# developer community, the .NET developer community, and the Stack Overflow community—for generously sharing their knowledge. And to all who, directly or indirectly, contributed to this work—thank you.

# Introduction

Delegates, events, and lambda expressions are at the heart of modern C# development. Once you understand them, you unlock a new level of flexibility, power, and elegance in your code. This compact guide makes these essential concepts approachable, practical, and even fun to learn. Inside the book, you'll discover

- **An interactive learning style** that feels like you're in a real classroom—asking questions, getting answers, and engaging with the material.

- **Plenty of review questions and exercises** to cement your understanding and boost your confidence.

- **Clean, simple examples** that strip away complexity so you can focus on mastering the ideas that matter most.

## Who Is This Book For?

This book assumes you already have a working knowledge of **C#** (and/or **.NET**) and know how to compile and run a C# application in **Visual Studio**. It does not cover beginner-level topics such as installing Visual Studio or writing a basic "Hello World" program—these are widely available elsewhere. This pocket guide goes straight to the point—**delegates, events, and lambda expressions**—with no time spent on beginner setup or basics.

INTRODUCTION

**In brief, you are ready for this book if you can answer "yes" to all the following:**

- Are you familiar with .NET, C#, and basic object-oriented concepts?
- Do you know how to set up your coding environment?
- Can you compile and run a C# program in Visual Studio?

**You may want to skip this book if you answer "yes" to any of the following:**

- Are you looking for a tutorial or reference book that covers all C# features in detail?
- Do you avoid Windows, Visual Studio, or .NET and prefer to code without them?

## How Is the Book Organized?

Here is a brief overview of the book's structure:

**Chapter 1** discusses delegates. It begins with custom delegates and their use in programs, then moves on to multicast delegates, built-in delegates (Func and Action), and anonymous methods. The chapter concludes with practical notes to deepen your understanding of delegates.

**Chapter 2** focuses on events. It starts with a simple publisher-subscriber model, gradually refining it according to standard event guidelines. You'll also learn how to chain events, followed by a set of helpful tips for working with them effectively.

**Chapter 3** covers lambda expressions, their various types, and how they are applied in different contexts.

**Chapter 4** provides some supplementary material to sharpen your programming skills. It explores advanced topics related to delegates and events, including covariance and contravariance, event accessors, and interface events. The chapter closes with a GUI application example analyzing a built-in Click event.

**Appendix A** suggests some useful references to help you expand your C# knowledge.

**Appendix B** provides a complete list of my published books that can further support your growth as a developer.

# Source Code

You can get the source code for all the examples from the publisher's website (https://github.com/Apress/Delegates-Events-and-Lambda-Expressions-in-C). A complete Visual Studio solution is provided for all chapters. Figure 1 shows how it appears in **Visual Studio Community 2022 (64-bit)—Preview Version 17.14.11 Preview 1.0** on a Windows 11 machine.

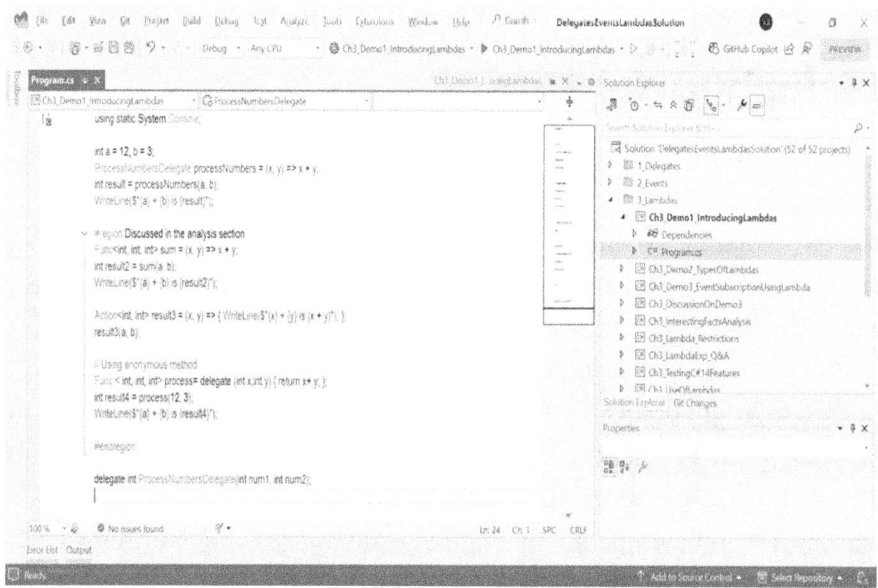

***Figure 1.*** *An example code (Demonstration 1 of Chapter 3) in Visual Studio Community 2022*

xix

INTRODUCTION

# Guidelines for Using This Book

To get the most out of your reading, I have the following suggestions:

- **Follow the sequence**—Reading the chapters in order will help you learn faster, as some related topics are introduced earlier and not repeated later.

- **Match the environment**—While the code examples should work in upcoming versions of C# and Visual Studio, software can be unpredictable. For consistent results, try to mimic the same setup used in this book.

- **Practice by typing**—All source code is available on the publisher's website. If you're using the digital edition, type the code yourself rather than copying and pasting—it's the best way to learn and avoid accidental errors.

# Useful Software

I began executing my programs using C# 13 and .NET 9 with **Visual Studio Community 2022**. You may also opt for Visual Studio Code, Microsoft's free, cross-platform source-code editor that runs on Windows, macOS, and Linux. If you prefer third-party tools such as JetBrains Rider, that should work as well—the choice is entirely yours.

As is often the case, software updates continued to roll out during the development of this book. I kept updating my setup and eventually switched to the **Preview** version. In the later stages, I worked with **.NET 10** and set the <LangVersion> to preview to experiment with specific **C# 14** features. When I completed my draft, my environment was running .NET SDK version **10.0.100-preview.4.25258.110**.

# INTRODUCTION

**Author's note:** The official link (Configure language version—C# reference | Microsoft Learn[1]) talks about how to set the language version in your project file.

The good news for you is that Visual Studio's community edition is free of cost. You can download and install the Visual Studio Preview from Visual Studio IDE Preview—Download and Test New Features.[2]

---

**Note**  By the time you have this book in your hands, it's quite possible that Visual Studio Community 2026 will have been released. At the time of writing, this link is functional, and the information is accurate. However, links and related policies may change in the future. This note applies to all links mentioned throughout this book.

---

## Conventions Used in This Book

Throughout this book, you will encounter numerous **"Q&A Sessions"** and **exercises**. Each question in the Q&A sessions is labeled using the format Q<Chapter_no>. <Question_no>. For example, **Q2.5** refers to *question 5 in Chapter 2*. Exercises follow a similar format—for example, **E3.2** refers to *exercise 2 in Chapter 3*.

All programs, outputs, and important notes in this book follow a consistent font and formatting style. In certain cases, important text is highlighted in **bold** to draw your attention. For example, consider the following code fragment (from Chapter 3):

---

[1] https://learn.microsoft.com/en-us/dotnet/csharp/language-reference/configure-language-version

[2] https://visualstudio.microsoft.com/vs/preview/#download-preview

xxi

## INTRODUCTION

```
using static System.Console;

Publisher publisher = new();
// Attaching an event handler
publisher.ValueChanged += Subscriber.HandleFlagValueChanged;
// Creating a new variable and attaching it as an event handler
EventHandler<FlagChangedEventArgs> FlagChanged = (sender, e) =>
{
 WriteLine($"The second handler: The flag value is changed to { e.Flag} ");
};
publisher.ValueChanged += FlagChanged;

// The remaining code is not shown here
```

I also want you to note that in many places, I have given you Microsoft's documentation links. Why? For me, as the creator, these are the authenticated sources of information to describe a feature.

# Final Words

Have you heard the ancient story of **Euclid** and **Ptolemy**, ruler of Egypt? When Ptolemy asked if there was an easier way to learn mathematics, Euclid replied, *"There is no royal road to geometry."* The same truth applies here—there's no shortcut to mastering programming. Read, experiment, and **write your own code**. Every challenge you face is an opportunity to grow. Each problem you solve will make you stronger and more confident as a developer.

**Errata**
While I've done my best to ensure accuracy, no book is perfect. That's why I maintain an Errata page where you can find any corrections or updates. Please check it from time to time.

**An Appeal**

Writing a quality book takes months, sometimes years. Authors like me depend on the support of our readers. If you find an illegal copy of this work, please let me or the Apress team know here: https://www.apress.com/gp/services/rights-permission/piracy. Your help makes a real difference.

**Share Your Feedback**

When you finish this book, I'd love to hear from you. Your reviews on Amazon or any other platform not only encourage me but also help fellow readers decide if this book is right for them.

# CHAPTER 1

# Delegates

Understanding delegates will help you flourish as a C# developer. This chapter attempts to simplify the topic.

## Concept

Delegates help you treat methods like objects. Let's recall the fundamentals of class and object. To create an object, say `calculator`, from a class `Calculator` (notice the C is in caps), you can write something like the following:

```
Calculator calculator = new();
```

Here, the object reference `calculator` points to an object of type `Calculator`. **Similarly, delegates are reference types, but instead of pointing to objects, they point to methods.** The official documentation Using Delegates - C# | Microsoft Learn[1] states the following about a delegate:

> A delegate is a type that safely encapsulates a method, similar to a function pointer in C and C++. Unlike C function pointers, delegates are object-oriented, type safe, and secure.

---

[1] https://learn.microsoft.com/en-us/dotnet/csharp/programming-guide/delegates/using-delegates

CHAPTER 1   DELEGATES

I assume that you know how to execute a method using the dot (.) operator. For example, when you use the line: `Console.WriteLine`, you instruct the `Console` type to invoke the `WriteLine` method. **Delegates provide an alternative way to execute a method.**

---
**POINT TO NOTE**

---

The dictionary definition of "delegate" is "a representative or an agent." Delegates in C# programming also represent methods with compatible signatures.

## Custom Delegates

In C# programming, you'll see both custom and built-in delegates. Once you're familiar with built-in delegates, you'd like to use them wherever possible. However, familiarity with the custom delegates will solidify your understanding. So, let's start our discussion with custom delegates.

## Defining a Delegate

The following code declares a delegate named `ProcessNumbersDelegate` that can encapsulate a method that takes two `int` arguments and returns `void`.

```
delegate void ProcessNumbersDelegate(int num1, int num2);
```

---
**POINT TO NOTE**

---

The general form to declare a delegate is as follows:

**<modifier> delegate <return type> (parameter list);**

You can see that this is similar to defining a method without a body.

Creating a delegate announces something like "This type of delegate can target/use any method that has these types of parameters and this return type."

## Assigning the Delegate Variable

To illustrate, let's assume that there is a class called `Calculator`. Assume that this class contains the following method:

```
public void DisplaySum(int num1, int num2)
{
    Console.WriteLine($"The sum of {num1} and {num2} is {num1 + num2}");
}
```

Since the signature (the return type and the parameter types) of the `DisplaySum` method matches the signature of the delegate `ProcessNumbersDelegate`, you can create a delegate instance by assigning the method to the delegate variable as follows:

```
ProcessNumbersDelegate processNumbers = calculator.DisplaySum;
```

**Author's note:** In this line of code, `calculator` is a `Calculator` object.

Notice that I created a variable (`processNumbers`) of the delegate type (`ProcessNumbersDelegate`) and assigned it a value that is nothing but the name of the method that matches the delegate. This flexibility offers useful benefits, such as changing method calls at run time or plugging new code into an existing class.

You may also note that I assigned an instance method to the delegate variable (`numberProcessorDelegate`) in this code segment. However, if needed, you can assign a static method as well (provided the method is accessible).

CHAPTER 1   DELEGATES

**Author's note:**

The following lines are equivalent:

```
ProcessNumbersDelegate processNumbers = calculator.DisplaySum;
ProcessNumbersDelegate processNumbers = new(calculator.DisplaySum);
ProcessNumbersDelegate processNumbers = newProcessNumbersDelegate
  (calculator.DisplaySum);
```

## Invoking the Delegate

You can invoke the delegate instance in the same way as a method. Here is a sample:

```
processNumbers(12, 3);
```

Upon executing this code, you'll see the following output:

```
The sum of 12 and 3 is 15
```

Let's see a complete program that covers all the key points that have been discussed so far.

## Demonstration 1

The following program shows you one static method (`DisplayTwoTimesTotal`) and two instance methods (`DisplaySum` and `DisplayDifference`). Let's use a custom delegate type (`ProcessNumbersDelegate`) instance to call these methods.

## CHAPTER 1  DELEGATES

---
### POINT TO NOTE
---

This book heavily uses top-level statements. Using this syntax, you can place the executable code at the top of your file, i.e., from line number 1. Hence, these are "top-level" statements. As a result, you can reduce code size by removing the Main method and its associated class. If you are new to it, I suggest you learn more about it from the online link: Top-level statements tutorial - C# | Microsoft Learn[2].

```
using static System.Console;

int a = 12, b = 3;
Calculator calculator = new();

// Assigning the delegate variable to an instance method
ProcessNumbersDelegate processNumbers = calculator.DisplaySum;
processNumbers(a, b); // Invoking the delegate

// Assigning the delegate variable to an instance method
processNumbers = calculator.DisplayDifference;
processNumbers(a, b); // Invoking the delegate

// Assigning the delegate variable to a static method
processNumbers= DisplayTwoTimesTotal;
processNumbers(a, b); // Invoking the delegate

static void DisplayTwoTimesTotal(int num1, int num2)
{
    WriteLine($"The result of ({num1} + {num2}) * 2 is {(num1 + num2) * 2}");
}

delegate void ProcessNumbersDelegate(int num1, int num2);
```

---

[2]https://learn.microsoft.com/en-us/dotnet/csharp/tutorials/top-level-statements

# CHAPTER 1  DELEGATES

```
class Calculator
{
    public void DisplaySum(int num1, int num2)
    {
        WriteLine($"The sum of {num1} and {num2} is {num1 + num2}");
    }
    public void DisplayDifference(int num1, int num2)
    {
        WriteLine($"The difference of {num1} and {num2} is {num1 - num2}");
    }
}
```

---

**Note** The top-level statements must precede namespace and type declarations. So, you see the delegate declaration and the Calculator class at the bottom of this program.

---

## Output

Upon executing this program, you'll get the following output:

```
The sum of 12 and 3 is 15
The difference of 12 and 3 is 9
The result of (12 + 3) * 2 is 30
```

## Analysis

This program demonstrates the following points:

- While the program was running, I could switch between three different methods. Interestingly, two of them were instance methods, and one of them was a static method. You saw that the delegate instance successfully invoked both types of methods.

- Even though I called processNumbers with the same arguments each time, the output was different. How was this possible? I changed the target methods on the fly.

## Q&A Session

**Q1.1 While matching the signatures of a delegate and a method, do I need to consider the return type?**

Yes. The official documentation Work with delegate types in C# - C# | Microsoft Learn[3] confirms this by saying:

> *In the context of method overloading, the signature of a method doesn't include the return value. However, in the context of delegates, the signature does include the return value. In other words, a method must have a compatible return type as the return type declared by the delegate.*

**Q1.2 In the previous Microsoft quote, I see the words "compatible return type" instead of "matching return type." Is there any specific reason for this?**

Yes. Once you learn about variances, you'll understand that the word "compatible" suits better than the word "matching" in this context. Many readers find the concept difficult at the initial phase of their learning. So, I have placed those discussions in Chapter 4. At this stage, it will be enough for you to remember the following information from the official documentation (see Variance in Delegates - C# | Microsoft Learn[4]):

---

[3] https://learn.microsoft.com/en-us/dotnet/csharp/programming-guide/delegates/
[4] https://learn.microsoft.com/en-us/dotnet/csharp/programming-guide/concepts/covariance-contravariance/variance-in-delegates

CHAPTER 1   DELEGATES

> .NET Framework 3.5 introduced variance support for matching method signatures with delegate types in all delegates in C#. This means that you can assign to delegates not only methods that have matching signatures, but also methods that return more derived types (**covariance**) or that accept parameters that have less derived types (**contravariance**) than that specified by the delegate type.

So, you can see that

- Covariance talks about the **return type compatibility.**
- Contravariance deals with the **parameter(s) compatibility.**

Now you understand that the word "compatible" suits better than the word "matching" in this context.

### Q1.3 How do delegates promote type safety?

Let's assume that the Calculator class (shown in Demonstration 1) has one more method as follows:

```
public void int DummyMethod()
{
  return 5;
}
```

However, the delegate variable processNumbers cannot point to this method. Why? Notice that the method signature and the delegate signature are different. So, the following line:

```
processNumbers = calculator.DummyMethod; // Error CS0123
```

will cause the following error:

```
CS0123 No overload for 'DummyMethod' matches delegate 'ProcessNumbersDelegate'
```

This shows you that delegates can help you promote type safety as well.

CHAPTER 1 DELEGATES

**Author's note:** This is why delegates are often referred to as *type-safe function pointers*. You can download the project Ch1_Q&A_On_Demo1 to verify the answer to Q1.3 and Q1.4 (the next question).

**Q1.4 In Demonstration 1, you have used the following line:**

```
ProcessNumbersDelegate processNumbers = calculator.DisplaySum;
```

**Now I'm worried. What will happen if I overload the DisplaySum method in the Calculator class?**

It does not matter. Delegates act like type-safe function pointers because they can track full method signatures (for example, number of parameters, type of parameters, and return type of methods) accurately. So, while using delegates, if you have overloaded methods, the compiler can bind the correct method for you. To investigate this, you can include an overloaded version of the DisplaySum method inside the Calculator class as follows:

```
public void DisplaySum(int num1, int num2,int num3)
{
   WriteLine($"The sum of {num1}, {num2} and {num2} is {num1 + num2 + num3}");
}
```

Now, if you execute the program again, you'll see that there is no change in the output.

So, it is also obvious that if you do not have the correct overloaded version, you'll receive a compile-time error. For example, if the Calculator class is as follows (see the correct overloaded method is commented out now):

```
class Calculator
{
    // public void DisplaySum(int num1, int num2)
    // {
    //    WriteLine($"The sum of {num1} and {num2} is {num1 + num2}");
    // }
```

```csharp
// Used in Q&A Session
public void DisplaySum(int num1, int num2, int num3)
{
   WriteLine($"The sum of {num1}, {num2} and {num2} is {num1 + num2 + num3}");
}
public void DisplayDifference(int num1, int num2)
{
   WriteLine($"The difference of {num1} and {num2} is {num1 - num2}");
}
}
```

You'll receive the following compilation error:

```
CS0123 No overload for 'DisplaySum' matches delegate 'ProcessNumbersDelegate'
```

# Multicasting

Each delegate instance has the multicast capability. This means that you can use a delegate instance to invoke multiple methods. Let's exercise this feature in this section.

## Working on Invocation List

To invoke multiple methods, the runtime maintains a list. **When a multicast delegate is called, the delegates in the list are executed in order.**

How to add a method to the delegate's invocation list? You need to use the + (or +=) operator. In this case, the delegates will be invoked following the order in which you add them to the chain. How to reduce the chain? You can drop the delegate method call by using the - (or -=) operator.

CHAPTER 1　DELEGATES

## Demonstration 2

A multicast delegate instance typically targets methods that have a `void` return type. To demonstrate the use of a multicast delegate, let us modify Demonstration 1 as follows:

```
using static System.Console;

int a = 12, b = 3;
Calculator calculator = new();

// Forming the chain with three delegate method calls
ProcessNumbersDelegate processNumbers = calculator.DisplaySum;
processNumbers += calculator.DisplayDifference;
processNumbers += DisplayTwoTimesTotal;
processNumbers(a, b);

// There is no change in the remaining code
```

**Author's note:** Since you have seen the `Calculator` class and the `ProcessNumbersDelegate` already in the previous demonstration, I did not repeat them here. You can download the *Ch1_Demo2_MulticastDelegate* project from the Apress website to see the complete program.

## Output

Upon executing this program, you'll see the following output:

```
The sum of 12 and 3 is 15
The difference of 12 and 3 is 9
The result of (12 + 3) * 2 is 30
```

You can see that it is the same output that you saw by executing Demonstration 1.

As said before, you can reduce the chain by dropping a delegate as follows:

```
processNumbers -= calculator.DisplayDifference;
```

11

CHAPTER 1   DELEGATES

To examine this, add the following code segment to this demonstration:

```
// There is no change in the previous code
WriteLine("Reducing the chain now.");
processNumbers -= calculator.DisplayDifference;
processNumbers(a, b);
// There is no change in the remaining code
```

If you now execute the program, you'll see the following output (see the new lines in bold):

```
The sum of 12 and 3 is 15
The difference of 12 and 3 is 9
The result of (12 + 3) * 2 is 30
Reducing the chain now.
The sum of 12 and 3 is 15
The result of (12 + 3) * 2 is 30
```

---

**CAUTION**

While targeting multiple methods using a multicast delegate, you need to be careful. If a method in your invocation list throws an exception, other methods will not get a chance to handle that exception.

---

## Alternative Code

In Demonstration 2, I have chained multiple **methods** in a delegate's invocation list. Here is an alternative code where I combine multiple **delegate instances** as well. For example, in this program (Demonstration 2), I could replace the following code (notice that I used one delegate variable to target three different methods):

```
ProcessNumbersDelegate processNumbers = calculator.DisplaySum;
processNumbers += calculator.DisplayDifference;
processNumbers += DisplayTwoTimesTotal;
processNumbers(a, b);
```

with the following code (see that now I use three delegate variables to target three different methods and chain them later using another variable) as well:

```
ProcessNumbersDelegate sum, diff, customCalculate, multidel;
sum = calculator.DisplaySum;
diff = calculator.DisplayDifference;
customCalculate = DisplayTwoTimesTotal;
multidel = sum + diff + customCalculate;
multidel(a, b);
```

| POINT TO REMEMBER |
|---|
| You can combine delegates if they are of the same type only. |

Once again, you'll see the same output by exercising this code. You can see that each method was called in the order that the delegate instances were added to the chain.

**Author's note:** You can download the *Ch1_Demo2_MulticastDelegate_Alternative* project from the Apress website to exercise the new code segment.

# Built-In Delegates

Interestingly, C# has many built-in delegates, some of which are very common. Let me talk about the Func and Action delegates now.

CHAPTER 1  DELEGATES

To target methods that accept zero or more input parameters (there are indeed a reasonable number of arguments) and have a return value, you'd use the Func delegates. If you target methods with a void return type, you'd use the Action delegates.

## Func Delegate

At the time of this writing, there are seventeen overloaded versions of the Func delegate. They can take 0 to 16 input parameters but always have one return type. See the following:

```
Func<out TResult>
Func<in T, out TResult>
Func<in T1, in T2, out TResult>
......
Func<in T1, in T2, in T3, in T4, in T5, in T6, in T7, in T8, in T9, in T10,
    in T11, in T12, in T13, in T14, in T15, in T16, out TResult>
```

> **POINT TO NOTE**
>
> The out parameter represents the **covariant return type,** and the in parameters represent the **contravariant parameter types**.

## Demonstration 3

To understand the usage, let's consider the following delegate:

```
delegate string PerformCalculationDelegate(int num1, int num2);
```

You understand that this delegate can target a method that takes two int arguments and returns a string. So, without declaring this custom delegate, you can use the built-in Func<int, int, string> delegate in your program.

CHAPTER 1　DELEGATES

To make things clear, the following program demonstrates the use of the custom delegate and its equivalent Func delegate as follows:

```
using static System.Console;

int a = 12, b = 3;
// Using the custom delegate
PerformCalculationDelegate calculate = GetTotal;
string result = calculate(a, b);
WriteLine(result);

// Using the built-in Func delegate
Func<int,int,string>  funcCalculate= GetTotal;
result = funcCalculate(a, b);
WriteLine(result);

string GetTotal(int x, int y)
{
    return $"{x} + {y} is {x + y}";
}
delegate string PerformCalculationDelegate(int num1, int num2);
```

## Output

Upon executing this program, you'll see the following output:

```
12 + 3 is 15
12 + 3 is 15
```

# Action Delegate

At the time of this writing, there are sixteen overloaded versions of the Action delegates. They can take 1 to 16 input parameters but do not have a return type. The overloaded versions are as follows:

```
Action<in T>
Action<in T1, in T2>
```

## CHAPTER 1    DELEGATES

```
Action<in T1, in T2, in T3>
....
Action<in T1, in T2, in T3, in T4, in T5, in T6, in T7, in T8, in
    T9, in T10, in T11, in T12, in T13, in T14, in T15, in T16>
```

To illustrate usage, you can refactor the code in Demonstration 1. For example, in that demonstration, you saw the following delegate:

```
delegate void ProcessNumbersDelegate(int num1, int num2);
```

Since the return type of the delegate was `void`, instead of using the following line in Demonstration 1:

```
// Assigning the delegate variable to an instance method
ProcessNumbersDelegate numberProcessorDelegate = new Calculator().DisplaySum;
```

you could use the built-in `Action<int, int>` delegate as follows:

```
Action<int, int> numberProcessorDelegate = calculator.DisplaySum;
```

---

### POINT TO NOTE

Now you know how built-in delegates can help you. Notice that the `Func` and the `Action` delegates are nothing but generic delegates. Since C# was originally introduced without generics, these built-in generic delegates did not exist in the earlier days.

While understanding custom delegates is very valuable, after completing this book, you'll likely prefer using built-in delegates (along with lambda expressions) wherever possible. The official documentation .NET Coding Conventions - C# | Microsoft Learn[5] also recommends using built-in `Func` and `Action` delegates, instead of defining delegate types.

---

[5] https://learn.microsoft.com/en-us/dotnet/csharp/fundamentals/coding-style/coding-conventions

However, it is also true that there are situations where you can use a custom delegate but not an equivalent Func or Action delegate.

## Q&A Session

**Q1.5 "A multicast delegate instance typically targets methods that have a void return type"—What is the reason behind this?**
A multicast delegate can indeed target multiple methods in its invocation list. However, if the methods have non-void return types, the delegate will only return the value from the **last method** in the list. The other methods are still called, but their return values are discarded.

**Q1.6 I understand that multicast delegates may not be useful for methods with a non-void return type because intermediate return values are discarded. But I believe that no one is preventing me from storing those values and using them in different ways. Is this correct?**
Yes. Though you can gather those values and use them as needed, you rarely need to do this. Also, at the time of this writing, there is no syntactical shortcut in C# to do this directly. If you use multicast delegates for methods with a non-void return type, the intermediate return values will be lost (i.e., a small part of functionality is not automatically preserved).

For example, if you execute the following code:

```
using static System.Console;

Func<int> del = GetOne;
del += GetTwo;

int result=del();
WriteLine($"The final value is { result}.");

static int GetOne()
{
    WriteLine("GetOne is executed.");
    return 1;
}
```

CHAPTER 1  DELEGATES

```
static int GetTwo()
{
    WriteLine("GetTwo is executed.");
    return 2;
}
```

You'll see the following output:

```
GetOne is executed.
GetTwo is executed.
The final value is 2.
```

You can see that both methods from the invocation list were called, but the final returned value is 2, which came from the GetTwo method.

**Author's note:** Download the **Ch1_Q1.6_Explanations** project to exercise this program.

**Q1.7 I can see that a delegate type can have generic type parameters. However, you did not discuss any custom generic delegate. Was this intentional?**

Generics are often considered an advanced topic. So, I started my discussion with non-generic custom delegates. Later, I discussed Func and Action delegates, which are the most common built-in generic delegates. They make programming easy. However, no one restricts you from using custom generic delegates. By following the construct of the built-in generic delegates, you can easily make custom generic delegates.

For example, in Demonstration 3, I used the Func delegate as follows:

```
Func<int,int,string> funcCalculate= GetTotal;
```

If you hover your mouse over Func, you'll see the following (see Figure 1-1):

CHAPTER 1   DELEGATES

```
delegate TResult System.Func<in T1, in T2, out TResult>(T1 arg1, T2 arg2)
    where T1 : allows ref struct
    where T2 : allows ref struct
    where TResult : allows ref struct
Encapsulates a method that has two parameters and returns a value of the type specified by the string parameter.

Returns:
    The return value of the method that this delegate encapsulates.

T1 is int
T2 is int
TResult is string
```

***Figure 1-1.*** *Retrieving the Func<int,int,string> details from Visual Studio*

Following this definition, you can define a custom generic delegate as follows:

```
delegate string CustomFuncDelegate<in T1,in T2,out TResult> (T1 num1, T2 num2);
```

And now you can use it as follows:

```
// Using custom generic delegate
CustomFuncDelegate<int, int, string> customFuncCalculate = GetTotal;
result = customFuncCalculate(a, b);
WriteLine(result);
```

**Q1.8 It appears to me that you could directly start the discussion on delegates using built-in Func and Action delegates. Is this correct?**

First, you'll see the use of custom delegates in many places. As said before, C# was introduced without generics. So, built-in generic delegates (such as `Func` and `Action`) were absent in the legacy code. Also, there are situations where you can use custom delegates but not built-in delegates.

**Q1.9 "There are situations where you can use custom delegates but not built-in delegates." Can you give an example?**

Those typical scenarios include the use of `ref`, `out`, and pointer parameters. For example, consider the following code that will work fine:

19

# CHAPTER 1  DELEGATES

```csharp
using static System.Console;

TryParseInt tryParseInt = IsValidInteger;

bool result = tryParseInt("10", out int num);
WriteLine($"Was the conversion successful? {result}");
WriteLine($"The number is {num}");

bool IsValidInteger(string inputString, out int number)
{
    bool flag = int.TryParse(inputString, out number);
    if (flag)
    {
        WriteLine($"Converted '{inputString}' to {number}.");
    }
    else
    {
        WriteLine($"Not a valid number.");
    }
    return flag;
}
delegate bool TryParseInt(string value1, out int value2);
```

And print the result:

```
Converted '10' to 10.
Was the conversion successful? True
The number is 10
```

However, instead of using the custom delegate, if you try to use a built-in delegate as follows:

```csharp
// The following line will raise a compile-time error
Func <string, out int, bool> parseFunction=IsValidInteger;
```

**This code will not compile.** This example demonstrates a situation where you can use a custom delegate that cannot be replaced with the corresponding built-in Func delegate.

**Author's note:** You can download the project, named **Ch1_Q1.9_CustomVsBuiltInDelegates**, to review this program.

# Anonymous Method

Instead of explicitly declaring and naming a delegate method, you can create an anonymous method. Typically, an anonymous method is a small inline function. You can use them to improve the readability of your code.

## Working on Anonymous Methods

Let's see an example. First, you declare the delegate the same way as you did earlier. Next, instead of writing a named function and assigning it to a delegate variable, you'd declare the function inline with no name.

### Demonstration 4

Here is a sample demonstration with the key segment in bold:

```
using static System.Console;

int a = 12, b = 3;

// Defining the function in-line
CalculateSumDelegate calculateSumDelegate = delegate (int x, int y)
{
    return $"The sum of {x} and {y} is {x + y}";
};
string result = calculateSumDelegate(a, b);
WriteLine(result);

delegate string CalculateSumDelegate(int num1, int num2);
```

CHAPTER 1   DELEGATES

## Output

Upon executing this program, you'll get the following output:

```
The sum of 12 and 3 is 15
```

Using the built-in Func delegate, you can simplify the program as follows:

```
using static System.Console;

int a = 12, b = 3;

// Defining the function in-line
Func<int, int, string> calculateSumDelegate = delegate (int x, int y)
{
    return $"The sum of {x} and {y} is {x + y}";
};
string result = calculateSumDelegate(a, b);
WriteLine(result);
```

> **POINT TO NOTE**
>
> Interestingly, the lambda expressions provide a more concise and expressive way to create an anonymous function. Once you complete Chapter 3, you'd like to make the previous code concise as follows:
>
> ```
> using static System.Console;
> int a = 12, b = 3;
> // Defining the function in-line
> Func<int, int, string> calculateSumDelegate = (x, y) => $"The sum of {x}
>     and {y} is {x + y}";
> string result = calculateSumDelegate(a, b);
> WriteLine(result);
> ```

CHAPTER 1  DELEGATES

## Q&A Session

**Q1.10 How does an anonymous method help me?**

Consider a case when your target method stays in a different location of the source file (or, in an extreme case, it is in a different source file). Such segregated codes are difficult to understand, debug, and maintain. In such situations, anonymous methods are helpful because you can define an "in-line" method without a name to serve your purpose directly where it's needed.

**Q1.11 "This chapter started with the line: "Understanding delegates will help you flourish as a C# developer." I'd love to hear more about this.**

Yes, understanding delegates helps you grasp and use many other powerful features in C#. For example, delegates are often used in callback methods (particularly in asynchronous programming). In the next chapter (Chapter 2), you will learn event handling, and there, you'll learn that events are built on delegates. You've also seen an example where I used a delegate variable with a lambda expression (the detailed discussion on this topic is included in Chapter 3) to make code shorter. You'll also find this knowledge beneficial while processing LINQ queries (not discussed in this book).

# Useful Notes

Before I conclude the chapter, let us analyze the following information.

CHAPTER 1   DELEGATES

# You Worked with a Sealed Class

The official documentation Using Delegates - C# | Microsoft Learn[6] states the following:

> Delegate types are derived from the Delegate class in .NET. Delegate types are sealed, they can't be derived from, and it isn't possible to derive custom classes from Delegate.

Now let's investigate the Intermediate Language (IL) code (it is also known as Common Language Runtime or CIL) of Demonstration 1. Here is a partial snapshot (see Figure 1-2):

```
// Assigning the delegate variable to a static method              ret
processNumbers= DisplayTwoTimesTotal;                         } // end of method Program::'<<Main>$>g__DisplayTwo
processNumbers(a, b); // Invoking the delegate
                                                              } // end of class Program
static void DisplayTwoTimesTotal(int num1, int num2)
{                                                             .class private auto ansi sealed ProcessNumbersDelegate
    WriteLine($"The result of ({num1} + {num2}) * 2 is {(num1 + num2)      extends [System.Runtime]System.MulticastDelegate
}                                                             {
                                                                // Methods
delegate void ProcessNumbersDelegate(int num1, int num2);       .method public hidebysig specialname rtspecialname
                                                                    instance void .ctor (
class Calculator                                                        object 'object',
{                                                                       native int 'method'
    public void DisplaySum(int num1, int num2)                      ) runtime managed
    {                                                               {
        WriteLine($"The sum of {num1} and {num2} is {num1 + num2}"); } // end of method ProcessNumbersDelegate::.ctor

    }                                                               .method public hidebysig newslot virtual
    public void DisplayDifference(int num1, int num2)                   instance void Invoke (
    {                                                                       int32 num1,
        WriteLine($"The difference of {num1} and {num2} is {num1 - nu        int32 num2
    }                                                                   ) runtime managed
}                                                                   {
                                                                    } // end of method ProcessNumbersDelegate::Invoke
```

***Figure 1-2.*** *The IL code of Demonstration 1*

**Author's note:** You can see the IL code in different ways. I often use https://sharplab.io/ to investigate the IL code.

Following the arrow tips, you can see that the C# compiler turned the delegate into a sealed class, called MulticastDelegate. So, if you write something like

---

[6] https://learn.microsoft.com/en-us/dotnet/csharp/programming-guide/delegates/using-delegates

24

```
class Sample : MulticastDelegate // Error
{
 // Some code
}
```

You'll see the compile-time error:

```
'Sample' cannot derive from special class 'MulticastDelegate'
```

**This means that custom classes cannot derive from the MulticastDelegate class as well.**

Let's keep on investigating the `MulticastDelegate` class. By following the definition of this class in Visual Studio, you can see the following:

```
public abstract class MulticastDelegate : Delegate
  {
    // The remaining code is not shown
```

You can see that the `MulticastDelegate` class derives from the `Delegate` class. This means that though **you cannot create a custom class that directly derives from the `Delegate` class (or from the MulticastDelegate class), the compiler is allowed to do this.**

## You Used a Shorthand Code

You can see the presence of the `Invoke` method in Figure 1-2. This method matches the delegate's signature. Interestingly, the following lines of code are equivalent:

```
processNumbers(a, b); // Invoking the delegate
processNumbers.Invoke(a,b); // The alternative way to invoke the delegate
```

Now you understand that `processNumbers(a, b);` is nothing but a shorthand for `processNumbers.Invoke(a, b);`.

# CHAPTER 1  DELEGATES

In the same way, if you investigate the IL code of Demonstration 2, you'll see that C# compiles the += and -=operations made on the delegate to the static Combine and Remove methods of System.Delegate class. This gives you the clue that the following program will compile as well:

```
using static System.Console;

int a = 12, b = 3;
Calculator calculator = new();

// Forming the chain with three delegate method calls
ProcessNumbersDelegate sum, diff, customCalculate, multidel;
sum = calculator.DisplaySum;
diff = calculator.DisplayDifference;
customCalculate = DisplayTwoTimesTotal;

// multidel = sum + diff + customCalculate;
multidel= (ProcessNumbersDelegate)Delegate.Combine(sum,diff,customCalculate);
multidel(a, b);

WriteLine("Reducing the chain now.");
// multidel -= diff; //OK
multidel = (ProcessNumbersDelegate)Delegate.Remove(multidel, diff); // OK too
multidel(a, b);

static void DisplayTwoTimesTotal(int num1, int num2)
{
    WriteLine($"The result of ({num1} + {num2}) * 2 is {(num1 + num2) * 2}");
}

// There is no change in the Calculator class, DisplayTwoTimesTotal method
// and the ProcessNumberDelegate declaration that you saw in
// Demonstration 1 and Demonstration 2
```

And output the following:

```
The sum of 12 and 3 is 15
The difference of 12 and 3 is 9
The result of (12 + 3) * 2 is 30
```

CHAPTER 1  DELEGATES

```
Reducing the chain now.
The sum of 12 and 3 is 15
The result of (12 + 3) * 2 is 30
```

**Author's note:** You can download the *Ch1_Demo2_UsefulNotes* project from the Apress website to see the complete program.

---

**Note** You'll find some additional discussions on delegates in Chapter 4.

---

## Summary

An instantiated delegate is an object. You can store it in a variable, pass it as a method parameter, assign it to a property, and return it from a method. When you use a delegate to invoke a method, at a high level, the overall process can be divided into two parts. In the first part, you (the caller) invoke the delegate, and in the second part, the delegate calls your target method. This mechanism decouples a caller from a target method. In brief, upon completion of this chapter, you'll find no problem answering the following questions:

- What is a delegate? How can you use it in your program?
- How can you chain delegates?
- How can you use custom delegates?
- How can you use built-in Func and action delegates?
- When should you use a custom delegate instead of a built-in delegate?
- How does an anonymous method help?
- How can delegates help your future learning?

CHAPTER 1   DELEGATES

# Exercise 1

Let's solve the following exercises.

---

**Note**   For all exercises in this book, you can assume that the following line: `using static System.Console;` has already been added at the top of each code segment.

---

### E1.1 A line of code is missing in this code segment that outputs: The square of 5 is 25.

```
ProcessNumberDelegate squareMaker = MakeSquare;
WriteLine($"The square of 5 is {squareMaker(5)}");
int MakeSquare(int x)
{
    return x * x;
}
// The missing line of code is here
```

**Can you fill the gap by adding the missing line?**

### E1.2 Can you compile the following code?

```
Func<int, int, void> calculate = delegate (int x, int y)
{
    WriteLine( $"{x} + {y} is {x + y}");
};
calculate(10, 2);
```

### E1.3 Predict the output:

```
int a = 2, b = 3;
Calculate calculate = Add;
calculate += Multiply;
calculate(a, ref b);
```

```csharp
void Add(int x, ref int y)
{
    x++;
    y++;
    WriteLine($"{x} + {y} is {x + y}");
}
void Multiply(int x, ref int y)
{
    WriteLine($"{x} * {y} is {x * y}");
}
delegate void Calculate(int a, ref int b);
```

## E1.4 Can you predict the output?

```csharp
CongratulateDelegate congratulate = PraiseSomeone;
PrintMessage("Kate", congratulate);

void PrintMessage( string name, CongratulateDelegate cdel)
{
    cdel(name);
}
void PraiseSomeone(string name)
{
    WriteLine($"Hello, {name}! Congratulations.");
}
delegate void CongratulateDelegate(string name);
```

## E1.5 Can you predict the output?

```csharp
var converter = GetConverter();
WriteLine(converter(23));

int MakeDouble(int number)
{
    return number * 2;
}
```

## CHAPTER 1   DELEGATES

```
int MakeTriple(int number)
{
    return number * 3;
}
Func<int,int> GetConverter()
{
    int random = new Random().Next(1, 10);
    Func<int,int> makeFold= MakeDouble;
    if (random % 2 != 0)
    {
        makeFold = MakeTriple;
    }
    return makeFold;
}
```

## E1.6 Can you compile the following code?

```
Func<Sample> initialize = delegate ()
{
    return new Sample();
};
_ = initialize();

class Sample
{
    public Sample()
    {
        WriteLine("Initializing the Sample class.");
    }
}
```

## E1.7 Can you compile the following code?

```
Action<string, string> combineStrings = delegate ( string s1, string s2 )
{
    WriteLine(s1+s2);
};
```

```
Action<int, int> addNumbers = delegate (int i1,int i2)
{
    WriteLine(i1+i2);
};
combineStrings += addNumbers;
```

**E1.8** You are aware that in a typical company, there are different employees with different income brackets. The tax slab also varies according to their yearly income. Assume that such a company has made a big profit, and the management decides to distribute the profit as a bonus among the employees. Since the bonus is also a part of yearly income, each employee needs to pay tax on this additional income as well. Let's make an application in which an employee can check the tax liability due to this bonus income.

There are different ways to make such an application. Since you have learned to use delegates in this chapter, I want you to use delegates in your application. To simplify things, let's assume that the company includes only three types of employees: junior, intermediate, and senior, who pay taxes at rates of 10%, 20%, and 30%, respectively, on their net income.

To make the problem statement clearer, here are some sample outputs from my implementation:

### Sample output-1:

```
Enter employee category (junior, intermediate, or senior):
intermediate
Enter the bonus amount (in USD):
1500
The employee needs to pay $300.0 in tax on the bonus income.
```

### Sample output-2:

```
Enter employee category (junior, intermediate, or senior):
junior
```

CHAPTER 1   DELEGATES

```
Enter the bonus amount (in USD):
1500
The employee needs to pay $150.0 in tax on the bonus income.
```

If you want, you can also handle invalid or negative inputs. Let's see two more sample outputs from my implementation as well:

### Sample output-3:

```
Enter employee category (junior, intermediate, or senior):
abc
Enter the bonus amount (in USD):
1000
Invalid employee type.
```

### Sample output-4:

```
Enter employee category (junior, intermediate, or senior):
junior
Enter the bonus amount (in USD):
xchh
The input string 'xchh' was not in a correct format.
```

**Can you make the application?**

# Keys to Exercise 1

Here is a sample solution set for the exercises in this chapter.

## E1.1

The delegate declaration was missing in the code segment. It is as follows:

```
delegate int ProcessNumberDelegate(int n);
```

CHAPTER 1   DELEGATES

# E1.2

No. You'll see the following error:

`CS1547 Keyword 'void' cannot be used in this context`

Notice that the method has a `void` return type. So, you can use the `Action` delegate as follows (notice the change in bold):

```
using static System.Console;
Action<int, int> calculate = delegate (int x, int y) // Correct
{
    WriteLine( $"{x} + {y} is {x + y}");
};
calculate(10, 2);
```

# E1.3

Here is the output:

```
3 + 4 is 7
2 * 4 is 8
```

**Additional note:** Notice that the delegate accepts a `ref` parameter, and b was passed as a reference variable. So, the changed value of b persisted before the multiplication operation.

# E1.4

Here is the output:

`Hello, Kate! Congratulations.`

Notice that you have passed the delegate variable as a method parameter.

CHAPTER 1    DELEGATES

## E1.5

The output depends on the generated random number. If it is an even number, you'll get 46 (i.e., 23*2). Otherwise, you'll get 69 (i.e., 23*3).

Note that the GetConverter method returned a delegate instance in this example.

## E1.6

Yes. This code will produce the following output:

```
Initializing the Sample class.
```

## E1.7

No. You are allowed to combine the delegates of the same type only. In this case, you'll see the following error:

```
CS0029    Cannot implicitly convert type 'System.Action<int, int>' to
  'System.Action<string, string>'
```

## E1.8

Here is a sample implementation:

```
using static System.Console;
try
{
    WriteLine("Enter employee category (junior, intermediate, or senior):");
    string type = ReadLine();

    WriteLine("Enter the bonus amount (in USD):");
    decimal bonusAmount = decimal.Parse(ReadLine());
    GetTaxInfo(type, bonusAmount);
}
```

```
catch(Exception e)
{
    WriteLine(e.Message);
}
void GetTaxInfo(string empType, decimal income)
{
    bool flag = true;
    Func<decimal, decimal> getTaxInfo = null;
    if (empType == "junior")
    {
        getTaxInfo = CalculateJuniorEmployeeTax;
    }
    else if (empType == "intermediate")
    {
        getTaxInfo = CalculateIntermediateEmployeeTax;
    }
    else if (empType == "senior")
    {
        getTaxInfo = CalculateSeniorEmployeeTax;
    }
    else
    {
        WriteLine("Invalid employee type.");
        flag = false;
    }
    if (flag)
    {
        WriteLine($"The employee needs to pay ${getTaxInfo(income)}
            in tax on the bonus income.");
    }
}
#region Calculate tax for different employees
decimal CalculateJuniorEmployeeTax(decimal income)
{
    return income * 0.1m;
}
```

## CHAPTER 1　DELEGATES

```
decimal CalculateIntermediateEmployeeTax(decimal income)
{
    return income * 0.2m;
}
decimal CalculateSeniorEmployeeTax(decimal income)
{
    return income * 0.3m;
}
#endregion
```

# CHAPTER 2

# Events

C# has an exciting feature called events. Interestingly, the backbone of events is delegates. Since you already learned delegates, you are ready to play with events. This chapter simplifies the concept with easy-to-understand examples.

## Concept

I assume that you are already familiar with different kinds of online forms. Let's consider a case when you start filing an online tax form or retrieving the performance details of a candidate in a competitive examination from the organizer's website. In any of these cases, when you clicked a button or selected a radio button, you probably noticed the meaningful changes in the UI layout. This kind of functionality can be made using events.

**How do events work?** Here, you notice a publisher-subscriber model where one class (or object) raises a notification (event) and one or multiple classes (or objects) listen to that notification. The object that raises the event is termed a **publisher** (or sender or broadcaster), and the object that receives the event is termed a **subscriber** (or a receiver).

A publisher may not care how the receivers interpret the events (or notifications). A subscriber can also decide when to start listening to events or when to stop listening to events. (In programming terms, you can say when to register for events and when to unregister from the events).

CHAPTER 2   EVENTS

---
**POINT TO NOTE**

---

You can relate this to Facebook or Twitter. If you follow someone, you can get notifications when that person posts an update. If you do not want to get notifications, you can always unsubscribe.

---

**Author's note:** In an event-driven architecture, you do not allow subscribers to communicate with each other. By doing this, you make a loosely coupled system.

## Designing a Publisher-Subscriber Model

Let's design a publisher-subscriber model and handle events. Before I start, let me acknowledge that the Visual Studio IDE can make your life easy when you deal with events. However, it's better to learn from the basics.

Let's begin with a simple program. I list the steps for an easy understanding:

- Step-1. Create a delegate. By convention, choose a delegate that has a name with the suffix `EventHandler`, something like the following:

    ```
    delegate void ValueChangedEventHandler(int x);
    ```

CHAPTER 2  EVENTS

---
**POINT TO NOTE**

---

Typically, the delegates used for events all have the `void` return type. You can verify this by examining the built-in delegates `EventHandler` or `EventHandler<TEventArgs>`, which are specifically designed to handle events. You can also see an interesting discussion about this topic at c# - Why do event handlers always have a return type of void? - Stack Overflow[1]

---

- Step-2. Following the convention, you can drop the suffix `EventHandler` from the delegate's name and set your event name as follows (you may note that I do not make the delegate `public`. As a result, other classes can subscribe to the event only through the event itself, not directly via the delegate type).

    ```
    public event ValueChangedEventHandler ValueChanged;
    ```

- Step-3. Declare a class that contains the event. This class also contains code to raise the event. **Interestingly, to trigger the event, you call the event like any other function.** Here is a sample code from the upcoming program:

    ```
    class Publisher
    {
        int flag = 0;
        // Declare the event
        public event ValueChangedEventHandler ValueChanged;
        public int Flag
        {
            get { return flag; }
    ```

---

[1] https://stackoverflow.com/questions/3325396/why-do-event-handlers-always-have-a-return-type-of-void

# CHAPTER 2 EVENTS

```
            set
            {
                flag = value;
                // Raise the event
                if (ValueChanged != null)
                {
                    ValueChanged(flag);
                }
            }
        }
    }
```

**Author's note:** You can see that I performed a null check before raising the event. Shortly, you'll see a discussion on this topic.

- Step-4. You can use an anonymous method or a lambda expression to handle the event. However, let's follow the common approach: create a class called Subscriber with a method to handle the event. This method should match the event's delegate signature. Here is a sample:

```
class Subscriber
{
    internal static void HandleFlagValueChanged(int value)
    {
        WriteLine($"The flag value is changed to {value}");
    }
}
```

- Step-5. Now you can attach the event handler to the publisher's event as follows:

```
publisher.ValueChanged += Subscriber.HandleFlagValueChanged;
```

# CHAPTER 2  EVENTS

**Author's note:** If the handler's signature does not match the event's delegate signature, you'll receive a compile-time error.

- Step-6. Similarly, you can detach the event handler from the publisher's event as follows:

```
publisher.ValueChanged -= Subscriber.HandleFlagValueChanged;
```

| POINTS TO REMEMBER |
|---|

Publisher is the type that contains the delegate. Subscribers register themselves by using += on the publisher's delegate and unregister themselves by using -= on that delegate. For events, these operators invoke the events `add` and `remove` accessors (a discussion on event accessors is added in Chapter 4). External code cannot directly read or assign the event; only the publisher can raise it. So, when we apply += or -= to an event, they have a special meaning (in other words, in those contexts, they are not shortcuts for the simple assignments).

## Demonstration 1

Let's verify all the discussed steps in the following demonstration:

```
using static System.Console;

Publisher publisher = new();
// Attaching an event handler
publisher.ValueChanged += Subscriber.HandleFlagValueChanged;
publisher.Flag = 1;
publisher.Flag = 2;
// Detaching the event handler
publisher.ValueChanged -= Subscriber.HandleFlagValueChanged;
publisher.Flag = 3;
```

CHAPTER 2  EVENTS

```
delegate void ValueChangedEventHandler(int x);
class Publisher
{
    int flag = 0;
    // Declare the event
    public event ValueChangedEventHandler? ValueChanged;
    public int Flag
    {
        get { return flag; }
        set
        {
            flag = value;
            // Raise the event
            if (ValueChanged != null)
            {
                ValueChanged(flag);
            }
            // Simplified form:
            // ValueChanged?.Invoke(flag);
        }
    }
}
class Subscriber
{
    internal static void HandleFlagValueChanged(int value)
    {
        WriteLine($"The flag value is changed to {value}");
    }
}
```

## Output

You'll receive the following output when you run this program:

```
The flag value is changed to 1
The flag value is changed to 2
```

## Analysis

When the value inside the `Publisher` class was changed to 1 or 2, the subscriber received notifications because it subscribed to the event. However, the subscriber unregistered himself before resetting the flag value to 3. So, there was no notification when the flag value was changed to 3.

## Q&A Session

**Q2.1 Why did you perform a null check before raising the event?**
It was necessary because raising an event without a handler causes a `NullReferenceException`.

**Q2.2 You could write a concise code to simplify the null check. Isn't it?**
Good catch. In fact, if you do several null checks like this, it'll make your code clumsy. So, you can avoid the **if** block by using the following code to make your program concise:

`ValueChanged?.Invoke(flag);`

**Q2.3 Why did you not use this concise code at the beginning?**
The null conditional operator was not available in earlier days; it came in C# 6. So, it is possible that you need to work with legacy code where this facility was not available. Secondly, while explaining steps in Demonstration 1, I told you that to trigger the event, you call the event like any other function. To demonstrate this, I used the code `ValueChanged(flag);` However, if you are not familiar with the `Invoke` function, the code `ValueChanged?.Invoke(flag);` could create confusion at that point of discussion in your mind.

**Q2.4 Can a publisher send a self-notification?**
Yes. Technically, you can use any method that matches the delegate signature as an event handler. To illustrate, let me add two methods in the `Publisher` class of Demonstration 1 as follows:

CHAPTER 2  EVENTS

```
class Publisher
{
    // There is no change in the previous/existing code
    // Used in Q&A
    public void NotifySelf(int newFlag)
    {
        WriteLine($"Self Notification: the new flag value is: {newFlag}");
    }
    public void NotifySelfAgain()
    {
        WriteLine($"Self Notification: the flag value is changed.");
    }
}
```

Since the signature of the NotifySelf method matches the delegate's (ValueChangedEventHandler) signature, you can write the following:

```
publisher.ValueChanged += publisher.NotifySelf; // OK
```

However, the signature of the NotifySelfAgain method does not match the delegate signature. So, the following line:

```
publisher.ValueChanged += publisher.NotifySelfAgain; // Error
```

will raise the following compile-time error:

```
CS0123 No overload for 'NotifySelfAgain' matches delegate 'ValueChangedEventHandler'
```

**Author's note:** You can download the project **Ch2_Q2.4** to verify the discussed code segments.

## Standard Event Guidelines

You can indeed write any event you desire. Developers follow their own coding styles. If the code is straightforward, there is no confusion. However, there are a few areas where individual coding styles can

# CHAPTER 2  EVENTS

create confusion. Interestingly, an event is a topic that belongs to such an area, and as a result, understanding event programming can be tough for many individuals (I faced this challenge as well). **This is why, following the standard guidelines, I'll gradually improve the previous implementation (Demonstration 1) and explain the changes in a particular implementation.** I am sure that once you read through these implementations, many of your confusions will be removed, and you'll find event programming truly interesting. Let's start.

The official link Handling and raising events - .NET | Microsoft Learn[2] states:

- Typically, to raise an event, you add a method that is marked as protected and virtual (in C#) or Protected and Overridable (in Visual Basic). The naming convention for the method is On<EventName>, such as OnDataReceived.

- The method should take one parameter that specifies an event data object, which is an object of type EventArgs or a derived type.

## First Update

Let's follow the official guidelines to make changes in the previous demonstration. Since I have not discussed EventArgs yet, let's focus on the first point now. As a first step, let's update the Publisher class as follows:

```
class Publisher
{
    int flag = 0;
    // Declare the event
    public event ValueChangedEventHandler? ValueChanged;
```

---

[2] https://learn.microsoft.com/en-us/dotnet/standard/events/

```
    public int Flag
    {
        get { return flag; }
        set
        {
            flag = value;
            OnValueChanged(flag);
        }
    }
    protected virtual void OnValueChanged(int currentValue)
    {
        if (ValueChanged != null)
        {
            ValueChanged(currentValue);
        }
        //// Simplified form
        // ValueChanged?.Invoke(currentValue);
    }
}
```

**Author's note:** If you run the application with this updated version of the Publisher class, you'll see the same output. You can download the project **Ch2_Demo1_FirstUpdate** to test this version of the code.

## Second Update

By following one of Microsoft's guidelines, you have incorporated some changes in the Publisher class. If you want to have component compatibility with .NET, you'd like to follow the other suggestion as well. In the previous implementation, the OnValueChanged method had an int parameter. **As per the official guideline, this method should accept a parameter of the EventArgs type or its derived type.**

## CHAPTER 2   EVENTS

If you investigate EventArgs from Visual Studio, you'll see the following:

```
using System.Runtime.CompilerServices;

namespace System
{
    // The base class for all event classes.
    [Serializable]
    [TypeForwardedFrom("mscorlib, Version=4.0.0.0,
      Culture=neutral, PublicKeyToken=b77a5c561934e089")]
    public class EventArgs
    {
        public static readonly EventArgs Empty = new EventArgs();

        public EventArgs()
        {
        }
    }
}
```

You can see that it is a class that has a static readonly field called Empty. If you do not wish to pass any data, you can pass **EventArgs.Empty**. However, in the previous examples, when the event was raised, you saw the changed values of the flag variable. So, we cannot pass EventArg.Empty in this implementation. To pass the data, let's make a derived class of EventArgs, called FlagChangedEventArgs, as follows:

```
class FlagChangedEventArgs : EventArgs
{
    public int Flag { get; }
    public FlagChangedEventArgs(int flag)
    {
        Flag = flag;
    }
}
```

CHAPTER 2    EVENTS

## MAKING THE CODE CONCISE

If you'd like to use the **primary constructor feature** (C#12 onwards), you can write the previous code as follows:

```
class FlagChangedEventArgs(int flag) : EventArgs
{
    public int Flag { get; } = flag;
}
```

**Author's note:** The subclass of EventArgs is typically named according to the information it provides (rather than the event for which it is created). So, if you reuse this class in the future, there will be no confusion about its purpose. In addition, notice that the Flag property does not have a setter in this code segment, i.e., it is read-only. It is because this kind of data is often exposed as properties or read-only fields.

It's time to see the Publisher class after introducing the changes:

```
class Publisher
{
    int flag = 0;
    // Declare the event
    public event ValueChangedEventHandler ValueChanged;
    public int Flag
    {
        get { return flag; }
        set
        {
            flag = value;
            OnValueChanged(new FlagChangedEventArgs(flag));
        }
    }
    protected virtual void OnValueChanged(FlagChangedEventArgs e)
```

48

```
    {
        if (ValueChanged != null)
        {
            ValueChanged(e.Flag);
        }
        // Simplified form:
        // ValueChanged?.Invoke(e.Flag);
    }
}
```

**Author's note:** You can download the project **Ch2_Demo1_SecondUpdate** to test this version of the code.

## Third Update

.NET event handlers have a specific form. Most of the time, you'll see the use of EventHandler and EventHandler<TEventArgs> to cover event scenarios. Let's investigate the details of the built-in generic delegate EventHandler<TEventArgs> from Visual Studio:

```
namespace System
{
    //
    // Summary:
    //     Represents the method that will handle an event when the event
    //     provides data.
    //
    //
    // Parameters:
    //   sender:
    //     The source of the event.
    //
    //   e:
    //     An object that contains the event data.
    //
```

```
    // Type parameters:
    //   TEventArgs:
    //     The type of the event data generated by the event.
    public delegate void EventHandler<TEventArgs>(object? sender, TEventArgs e);
}
```

The method summary is self-explanatory. By seeing this delegate signature, you can get a clue that the event handlers in .NET have the following form:

```
void EventHandlerMethod (object? sender, TEventArgs e) {
  // some code
}
```

> **POINT TO NOTE**
>
> In the previous method, **the first parameter is used to identify the source of the event, and it is always of type object.** Typically, the calling code passes `this` for the sender parameter. You have already learned that **the second parameter is used to pass the event data.** If you do not wish to pass any data, you can pass `EventArgs.Empty`.

To make a .NET-compatible version of that program, let's improve the previous implementation(s).

## Demonstration 2

Till now, I have been modifying the initial implementation. So, the previous programs keep showing the changed values only. This time onward, let's print the source of the notification as well. Here is an updated implementation for the previous demonstrations:

```
using static System.Console;

Publisher publisher = new();
// Attaching an event handler
publisher.ValueChanged += Subscriber.HandleFlagValueChanged;
publisher.Flag = 1;
publisher.Flag = 2;
// Detaching the event handler
publisher.ValueChanged -= Subscriber.HandleFlagValueChanged;
publisher.Flag = 3;
```
**delegate void ValueChangedEventHandler(object? sender, FlagChangedEventArgs e);**
```
class FlagChangedEventArgs : EventArgs
{
    public int Flag { get; }
    public FlagChangedEventArgs(int flag)
    {
        Flag = flag;
    }
}

class Publisher
{
    int flag = 0;
    // Declare the event
    public event ValueChangedEventHandler? ValueChanged;
    public int Flag
    {
        get { return flag; }
        set
        {
            flag = value;
            OnValueChanged(new FlagChangedEventArgs(flag));
        }
    }
    protected virtual void OnValueChanged(FlagChangedEventArgs e)
    {
```

## CHAPTER 2   EVENTS

```
        if (ValueChanged != null)
        {
            ValueChanged(this, e);
        }
        //// Simplified form:
        // ValueChanged?.Invoke(this, e);
    }
}
class Subscriber
{
    internal static void HandleFlagValueChanged(object? sender,
      FlagChangedEventArgs e)
    {
        // WriteLine($"The flag value is changed to {value}");
        // Prints the source of notification as well
        WriteLine($"The flag value in {sender} is changed to {e.Flag}");
    }
}
```

## Output

There is no surprise that you'll see the following output when you run this program:

```
The flag value in Publisher is changed to 1
The flag value in Publisher is changed to 2
```

**Author's note:** I remind you that since the subscriber unregistered himself before resetting the flag value to 3, there was no notification when the flag value was changed to 3.

CHAPTER 2   EVENTS

# Final Update

Many events in .NET Framework indeed follow the non-generic custom delegate pattern to support backward compatibility. However, the official doc Handling and raising events - .NET | Microsoft Learn[3] now suggests the following:

> *Use the EventHandler delegate for all events that don't include event data. Use the EventHandler<TEventArgs> delegate for events that include data about the event.*

# Demonstration 3

If you'd like to follow this suggestion, you'd need to replace the custom event delegate in the previous program with the built-in generic delegate called EventHandler<TEventArgs>. To implement the idea, you only need to bring the changes to the Publisher class. Let's see the following program with the key changes in bold:

```
using static System.Console;

Publisher publisher = new();
// Attaching an event handler
publisher.ValueChanged += Subscriber.HandleFlagValueChanged;
publisher.Flag = 1;
publisher.Flag = 2;
// Detaching the event handler
publisher.ValueChanged -= Subscriber.HandleFlagValueChanged;
publisher.Flag = 3;

// The custom delegate is no longer needed
// There is no change in the FlagChangedEventArgs class as well
```

---

[3] https://learn.microsoft.com/en-us/dotnet/standard/events/

## CHAPTER 2 EVENTS

```
class Publisher
{
    int flag = 0;
    // Declare the event
    // public event ValueChangedEventHandler? ValueChanged;
    public event EventHandler<FlagChangedEventArgs>? ValueChanged;
    public int Flag
    {
        get { return flag; }
        set
        {
            flag = value;
            OnValueChanged(new FlagChangedEventArgs(flag));
        }
    }
    protected virtual void OnValueChanged(FlagChangedEventArgs e)
    {
        if (ValueChanged != null)
        {
            ValueChanged(this, e);
        }
        //// Simplified form:
        // ValueChanged?.Invoke(this, e);
    }
}
// There is no change in the Subscriber class that you saw in
// the previous demonstration (Demonstration 2).
```

**Author's note:** To execute the complete program, you can download the project **Ch2_Demo3_UsingEventHandler** from the Apress website.

## Output

Once again, upon executing the program, you'll see the same output that you saw in Demonstration 2. So, I'd not repeat it here.

CHAPTER 2    EVENTS

---
**POINT TO NOTE**

---

While raising events, you may not need to pass any additional information. In such cases, you can use the non-generic delegate `EventHandler`. The E2.3 of Exercise 2 will demonstrate its usage.

## Q&A Session

**Q2.5 I see that you are always detaching the event handlers before closing the programs. Is this necessary?**
If you subscribe to an event, you should also unsubscribe from it before you close the application to avoid memory leaks. In a simple application, you may not see the impact. However, in an enterprise application, memory leaks are one of the biggest concerns.

# Chaining Events

Multiple objects may respond to an event notification. This means that you may need to work with multicast events. Similar to delegates, you can chain events using the += operator.

# Adding More Handlers

To verify this, let's add two more handlers to the previous program. One of the handlers is added to the `Subscriber` class, and the other one is added as an **anonymous delegate**.

**Author's note:** While adding the third handler as an anonymous delegate, I have marked two code segments as "Recommended Practice" and "Bad Practice." Currently, the code segment that is marked with "Recommended section" is intentionally commented. Shortly, you'll see the in-depth discussions on these code segments.

55

CHAPTER 2  EVENTS

# Demonstration 4

Let's see the following program with the key changes in bold:

```
using static System.Console;

Publisher publisher = new();
// Attaching an event handler
publisher.ValueChanged += Subscriber.HandleFlagValueChanged;
// Attaching the second event handler
publisher.ValueChanged += Subscriber.SecondHandlerForFlagValueChanged;

#region Bad practice
// Attaching the third event handler
publisher.ValueChanged += delegate (object? sender, FlagChangedEventArgs e)
{
    WriteLine($"Got notification: {sender}'s flag value is changed to {e.Flag}");
};
#endregion

#region Recommended practice
//// Attaching the third event handler
// EventHandler<FlagChangedEventArgs> temp = delegate (object?
// sender, FlagChangedEventArgs e)
// {
//     WriteLine($"Got notification: {sender}'s flag value is changed to {e.Flag}");
// };
// publisher.ValueChanged += temp;
#endregion

publisher.Flag = 1;
publisher.Flag = 2;

// Detaching event handlers
publisher.ValueChanged -= Subscriber.HandleFlagValueChanged;
publisher.ValueChanged -= Subscriber.SecondHandlerForFlagValueChanged;

publisher.Flag = 3;
```

```csharp
class FlagChangedEventArgs : EventArgs
{
    public int Flag { get; }
    public FlagChangedEventArgs(int flag)
    {
        Flag = flag;
    }
}
class Publisher
{
    int flag = 0;
    // Declare the event
    public event EventHandler<FlagChangedEventArgs>? ValueChanged;
    public int Flag
    {
        get { return flag; }
        set
        {
            flag = value;
            OnValueChanged(new FlagChangedEventArgs(flag));
        }
    }
    protected virtual void OnValueChanged(FlagChangedEventArgs e)
    {
        if (ValueChanged != null)
        {
            ValueChanged(this, e);
        }
    }
}
class Subscriber
{
    internal static void HandleFlagValueChanged(object? sender,
      FlagChangedEventArgs e)
```

## CHAPTER 2  EVENTS

```
    {
        // Prints the source of notification as well
        WriteLine($"The flag value in {sender} is changed to {e.Flag}");
    }
    internal static void SecondHandlerForFlagValueChanged(object? sender,
      FlagChangedEventArgs e)
    {
        WriteLine($"Second Handler: the flag value in {sender} is changed to
         { e.Flag} ");
    }
}
```

## Output

Upon executing the program, you'll see the following output:

```
The flag value in Publisher is changed to 1
Second Handler: the flag value in Publisher is changed to 1
Got notification: Publisher's flag value is changed to 1
The flag value in Publisher is changed to 2
Second Handler: the flag value in Publisher is changed to 2
Got notification: Publisher's flag value is changed to 2
Got notification: Publisher's flag value is changed to 3
```

## Analysis

You can see that when the flag value was changed to 1 or 2, all the handlers were notified. However, before changing the flag value to 3, two of the subscribers unregistered themselves. So, when the flag value was changed to 3, only the third handler (see the anonymous delegate) got the notification.

## Q&A Session

**Q2.6 I see lots of similarities between delegates and events. For example, both have single-cast and multicast capabilities, and they use similar syntax to add and remove handlers. Most importantly, invoking a delegate and raising an event are very similar. Am I correct?**

CHAPTER 2  EVENTS

I appreciate your observations. You are right.

> **DELEGATES VERSUS EVENTS**
>
> There are lots of similarities between delegates and events. This is why, while designing an application, new developers often struggle to decide whether to choose a design based on delegates or a design based on events. If you have the same doubt, I suggest you read the official documentation from the following link: Delegates vs. events - C# I Microsoft Learn[4]. Microsoft acknowledges that these are not hard and fast rules, but they will give you some meaningful insights.

# Useful Notes

Before I conclude the chapter, I'd like you to keep the following points in mind.

# Be Careful Before Using the Anonymous Method

There was no surprise in the output of the previous program. Let me remind you that to avoid memory leaks, once you subscribe to an event, you should also unsubscribe from it before you close the application. So, it makes sense to remove the third event handler in Demonstration 4 as well. Now the question is: how can you do this?

Let's assume that you have introduced the following code (shown in bold) before you set the flag value 3 in the previous demonstration: application:

---

[4] https://learn.microsoft.com/en-us/dotnet/csharp/distinguish-delegates-events

## CHAPTER 2   EVENTS

```
// There is no change in the previous code

// Detaching event handlers
publisher.ValueChanged -= Subscriber.HandleFlagValueChanged;
publisher.ValueChanged -= Subscriber.SecondHandlerForFlagValueChanged;
// There is no guarantee that the following code will detach
// the handler
publisher.ValueChanged -= delegate (object? sender, FlagChangedEventArgs e)
{
    WriteLine($"Unsubscribing the event");
};

publisher.Flag = 3;
// There is no change in the remaining code
```

**However, there is no guarantee that the compiler will unsubscribe this handler**. For example, upon executing this modified program on my computer, I can still see the following output **in which the last line was supposed to be absent:**

```
The flag value is changed to 1
The second handler notices that the flag value is changed to 1
Got notification: Publisher's flag value is changed to 1
The flag value is changed to 2
The second handler notices that the flag value is changed to 2
Got notification: Publisher's flag value is changed to 2
```
**Got notification: Publisher's flag value is changed to 3**

To avoid this, you can store the anonymous method in a delegate variable. As a result, while you attach (or detach) an event handler, you can keep track of it. Here is a sample code for attaching the handler:

```
#region Recommended practice
// Attaching the third event handler
EventHandler<FlagChangedEventArgs> temp = delegate (object? sender,
   FlagChangedEventArgs e)
```

60

```
{
    WriteLine($"Got notification: {sender}'s flag value is changed to
      {e.Flag}");
};
publisher.ValueChanged += temp;
#endregion
```

Now you can detach it following the usual process:

```
publisher.ValueChanged -= temp;
```

If you exercise these code segments, everything seems to be working again. Now you understand why I marked this code region as "Recommended practice" in Demonstration 4.

## Event Modifiers

The official link The `event` keyword - C# reference | Microsoft Learn[5] confirms that you can apply `public`, `private`, `protected`, `internal`, `protected internal`, or `private protected` modifiers to an event. It is also useful to note that events can be `virtual`, `abstract`, `sealed`, or `static` as well.

---

**Note** You'll find some additional discussions on events in Chapter 4.

---

## Summary

Events are one of the exciting features of advanced C#. Using events, you can send notifications from one part of your code to another. This chapter showed you many implementations and discussed the standard guidelines for programming events. In brief, this chapter discussed the following:

---

[5] https://learn.microsoft.com/en-us/dotnet/csharp/language-reference/keywords/event

# CHAPTER 2   EVENTS

- What is an event? How can you use it in your program?
- How can you use the built-in EventHandler and EventHandler<TEventArgs> in your program?
- How can you pass data while sending an event?
- How can you chain events?
- How should you use an anonymous method as an event handler?

and many more...

# Exercise 2

Let's solve the following exercises.

**E2.1 In Demonstration 1, you saw the use of a custom delegate. Can you write an equivalent program using a built-in delegate?**

**E2.2 In Demonstration 3, you declared the event as follows:**

```
public event EventHandler<FlagChangedEventArgs>? ValueChanged;
```

**Can you write equivalent code using an Action delegate?**

**E2.3 Can you predict the output of the following code?**

```
using static System.Console;

Publisher publisher = new();
// Attaching an event handler
publisher.ValueChanged += delegate (object? sender, EventArgs e)
{
    WriteLine($"The flag value is changed in {sender}");
};
publisher.Flag = 1;
class Publisher
{
    int flag = 0;
```

```
    // Declare the event
    public event EventHandler? ValueChanged;
    public int Flag
    {
        get { return flag; }
        set
        {
            flag = value;
            OnValueChanged();
        }
    }
    protected virtual void OnValueChanged()
    {
        if (ValueChanged != null)
        {
            ValueChanged(this, EventArgs.Empty);
        }
    }
}
```

**E2.4 State True/False:**

**i) Events rely on delegates to accomplish a task.**

**ii) You can attach any method to a specific event.**

**E2.5 Many private sector banks provide special facilities for their elite customers. However, a customer must maintain a healthy balance to qualify as an elite customer. Let's model this scenario with a toy application where a bank considers only $500 as a minimum balance to tag someone as an elite customer. You know that any customer can do an arbitrary number of deposits (or withdrawals). Let's assume that after each financial transaction, if the account balance is $500 or more, the bank will inform the customer whether he/she is an elite customer.**

CHAPTER 2   EVENTS

### Here is a sample output to give you an idea:

```
Enter amount (Type exit to quit application):
235.5
Current balance is 235.5
Enter amount (Type exit to quit application):
125
Current balance is 360.5
Enter amount (Type exit to quit application):
303.7
Current balance is 664.2
Currently, you are an elite customer for us.
Enter amount (Type exit to quit application):
-234
Current balance is 430.2
Enter amount (Type exit to quit application):
120.35
Current balance is 550.55
Currently, you are an elite customer for us.
Enter amount (Type exit to quit application):
exit
```

### Can you make such an application?

**Author's note:** For simplicity, you do not need to emphasize exception handling scenarios too much. Also, instead of using separate methods for deposits and withdrawals, you can use a single method (e.g., UpdateBalance) where, to withdraw an amount, you pass a negative value. However, both assumptions are optional for you.

# Keys to Exercise 2

Here is a sample solution set for the exercises in this chapter.

## E2.1

By seeing the custom delegate's signature, you understand that it is easy to replace its usage using `Action<int>`. Let me show you the code fragment (notice that the old code is commented out and the new code is shown in bold):

```
// There is no change in the previous code

publisher.Flag = 3;

// delegate void ValueChangedEventHandler(int x);
class Publisher
{
    int flag = 0;
    // Declare the event
    // public event ValueChangedEventHandler ValueChanged;
    public event Action<int>? ValueChanged;
    // There is no change in the remaining code
```

**Author's note:** Download the project Ch3_Ex1.1_UsingGenericActionDelegate to see/execute the complete program.

## E2.2

Here is an equivalent line of code:

```
public event Action<object?, FlagChangedEventArgs>? ValueChanged;
```

## E2.3

Here is the output:

```
The flag value is changed in Publisher
```

**Author's note:** This code sample shows a use of the non-generic `EventHandler`. Notice that while invoking the event, you passed `EventArgs.Empty`.

CHAPTER 2    EVENTS

# E2.4

See the answers inline.

i) Events rely on delegates to accomplish a task. [**True**]

ii) You can attach any method to a specific event. [**False**]

# E2.5

Here is a sample application:

```
using static System.Console;

Bank bank = new();
bank.BalanceChanged += BalanceChecker.MarkElite;

string input;
#region user input
try
{
    do
    {
        WriteLine("Enter amount (Type exit to quit application):");
        input = ReadLine();
        if (input != "exit")
        {
            bank.UpdateBalance(decimal.Parse(input));
        }
    } while (input != "exit");
}
catch(Exception e)
{
    WriteLine($"Error: {e}");
}
finally
{
```

CHAPTER 2  EVENTS

```
        // Detaching the event
        bank.BalanceChanged -= BalanceChecker.MarkElite;
    }
#endregion

class BalanceChecker
{
    public static void MarkElite(object? sender, BalanceChangedEventArgs e)
    {
        WriteLine($"Current balance is {e.CurrentBalance}");
        if (e.CurrentBalance >= 500.0m)
        {
            Write($"Currently, you are an elite customer for us.\n");
        }
    }
}
class BalanceChangedEventArgs : EventArgs
{
    public decimal CurrentBalance;
}
class Bank
{
    private decimal _balance = 0.0m;
    public event EventHandler<BalanceChangedEventArgs>? BalanceChanged;

    // For withdrawal, pass a negative amount
    public void UpdateBalance(decimal amount)
    {
        _balance += amount;
        OnBalanceChanged(_balance);
    }
    protected virtual void OnBalanceChanged(decimal currentBalance)
    {
```

```
            BalanceChangedEventArgs data = new()
            {
                CurrentBalance = currentBalance
            };
            BalanceChanged?.Invoke(this, data);
        }
    }
```

## CHAPTER 3

# Lambda Expressions

The inclusion of lambda expressions (often termed as lambdas) enhanced the C# programming language. These are powerful alternatives to anonymous methods. C# 2.0 introduced anonymous methods, and C# 3.0 introduced lambda expressions. Nowadays, lambda expressions are more popular than anonymous methods. Why? They are typically a perfect fit for inline declarations, more expressive, and easier to read. You often see lambda expressions while working with delegates, events, and LINQ. Since this pocketbook focuses on delegates and events, this chapter analyzes the uses of lambda expressions in those contexts.

---

**POINT TO NOTE**

The lambda expressions and anonymous methods are collectively known as *anonymous functions*.

---

## Concept

The name 'lambda' came from lambda calculus, which can be used to simulate a Turing machine. You spell it with the Greek letter lambda ($\lambda$), but your keyboard does not have it. So, to denote a lambda operator, you use the symbol =>. The left side of the operator specifies the input parameters (if any), and the right side of the operator specifies either an expression or a statement block. The => is right associative, and its precedence is the same as =. While reading the code that contains the lambda operator, you replace the lambda operator with **'goes to'** or **'go to'** or **'arrow' or become(s)**. For example, you read x=> x+5; as x goes to x+5. Similarly, you read (x,y)=>x+y; as x and y go to x+y.

## Programming Lambda Expressions

After defining a delegate signature, you can make a variable of the delegate type and write the lambda expression using the arrow operator (equal sign with a right-angle bracket).

### Demonstration 1

Here is a sample program:

```
using static System.Console;
int a = 12, b = 3;
ProcessNumbersDelegate processNumbers = (x, y) => x + y;
int result=processNumbers(a,b);
WriteLine($"{a} + {b} is {result}");

delegate int ProcessNumbersDelegate(int num1, int num2);
```

### Output

You'll receive the following output when you run this program:

```
12 + 3 is 15
```

CHAPTER 3  LAMBDA EXPRESSIONS

# Analysis

Since you are familiar with built-in delegates, you can understand that I could write an equivalent program as follows:

```
using static System.Console;

int a = 12, b = 3;
Func<int, int, int> sum = (x, y) => x + y;
int result2 = sum(12, 3);
WriteLine($"{a} + {b} is {result2}");
```

Why did I use the `Func` delegate in the previous segment? Notice that the target method had a return type. If the method does not have a return type, you can use an `Action` delegate. Let's see the following program:

```
using static System.Console;
int a = 12, b = 3;
Action<int, int> result3 = (x, y) => { WriteLine($"{x} + {y} is {x + y}"); };
result3(a, b);
```

**Author's note:** Once you download the **Ch3_Demo1_IntroducingLambdas** project, you'll see all these program segments. There is no surprise that each of these programs will print: 12 + 3 is 15.

---
**POINT TO NOTE**

---

When a lambda expression is converted to a delegate type, the result depends on the input parameters and return type. If a lambda expression doesn't have a return type, it can be converted to one of the `Action` delegate types. If it has a return type, it can be converted to one of the `Func` delegate types. `Func` and `Action` are generic delegates, which you learned about in Chapter 2.

71

# CHAPTER 3 LAMBDA EXPRESSIONS

## Q&A Session

**Q3.1 Can I have a lambda expression with an empty list of input parameters?**

Yes. See the following example:

```
using static System.Console;

Action say = () => WriteLine("Hello, reader!");
say();
```

Upon executing this program, you'll see the output:

```
Hello, reader!
```

**Author's note**: In Demonstration 1, you saw the lambda expression that accepts two parameters, and there you saw me using the parentheses as follows:

```
(x, y) => x + y;
```

If you use a lambda expression that has only one parameter, you can omit the parentheses. For example, the following line of code is valid as well (see the lambda expression without parentheses):

```
Func<int, int> square = x => x * x;
```

The use of the delegate operator gives you the flexibility of omitting the parameter list. So, there is no problem if you write something like the following:

```
Action say = delegate { WriteLine("Hello, reader!"); };
```

However, the lambda expression does not have this facility. For example, though you can write an equivalent code using the following line:

```
Action say = () => WriteLine("Hello, reader!");
```

You cannot avoid the empty parameter list. **This is the only functionality of anonymous methods that isn't supported by lambda expressions.**

## Q3.2 What is a Turing machine?

A Turing machine is an abstract machine that can manipulate symbols on a tape following some rules. It provides the mathematical foundation for computation, which underlies modern programming languages. It was invented by Alan Mathison Turing in 1936.

**Author's note:** The ACM A. M. Turing Award is often recognized as the highest honor[1] in the field of computer science; it is named after Alan Mathison Turing.

## Q3.3 It appears to me that I can omit the type declaration in a lambda expression. Is this correct?

If you do not supply parameters, the compiler tries to infer the type. However, sometimes the compiler can't infer those types. In that case, you need to supply the parameter(s). In this context, remember that the input parameters must be all implicit or explicit.

## Q3.4 "Input parameters must be all implicit or explicit." What does it mean?

Let's take an example. Consider the following code:

```
Action<string, int> printInfo = (name, age) => WriteLine($"Hello {name}. You are now {age}.");
printInfo("Kate", 25);
```

Or the following code:

```
var printInfo = (string name, int age) => WriteLine($"Hello {name}. You are now {age}.");
printInfo("Kate", 25);
```

Each of these code segments can output:

```
Hello Kate. You are now 25.
```

---

[1] https://en.wikipedia.org/wiki/Turing_Award

## CHAPTER 3  LAMBDA EXPRESSIONS

### However, if you try executing the following code:

```
var printInfo = (name, age) => WriteLine($"Hello {name}. You are now {age}.");
printInfo("Kate", 25);
```

### You'll see the compile-time error:

```
CS8917 The delegate type could not be inferred.
```

So, you understand that the input parameters must be all implicit or explicit.

**Author's note:** You can download the *Ch3_LambdaExp_Q&A* project to verify the code fragments that are discussed in Q3.1 and Q3.4.

# Types of Lambdas

There are two types of lambda expressions:

**Expression lambda**: It has the following form:

```
(input-parameters) => expression
```

**Statement lambda:** In the case of statement lambda, you may notice the use of curly braces, semicolons, and the return statement. A statement lambda can contain any number of statements, but in general, they contain two or three statements. A statement lambda may look like the following:

```
(input-parameters) =>
{
 Statement-1;
 Statement-2;
   ...
};
```

## Executing Different Lambdas

Let's execute a sample program that uses both kinds of lambdas.

## Demonstration 2

Here is a sample program that shows the usage of an expression lambda and a statement lambda. These two lambdas are equivalent in terms of functionality:

```
using static System.Console;

// Using an expression lambda
Func<int, int> expr_processor = x => x + 5;
WriteLine(expr_processor(3));

// Using a statement lambda
Func<int, int> stmt_processor = x =>
{
    int temp = x + 5;
    return temp;
};
WriteLine(stmt_processor(3));
```

## Output

Upon executing this program, you'll see that both lambda expressions add 5 to 3, producing the final result 8 as follows:

```
8
8
```

## Q&A Session

### Q3.5 What is an expression?

The official link https://learn.microsoft.com/en-us/dotnet/csharp/language-reference/language-specification/expressions states that an expression is a sequence of operators and operands.

CHAPTER 3  LAMBDA EXPRESSIONS

Typically, you can evaluate an expression to a single value, method, object, or namespace. An expression can also include a method call, an operator with the operands, a literal value (a literal is a constant value that does not have a name), or simply a name of a variable, type member, method parameter, namespace, or type. Consider the following statement:

```
int flag=1;
```

Here, `flag` is a simple name, and 1 is the literal value. Literals and simple names are the two simplest types of expression.

**Q3.6 It appears to me that, similar to a normal method, a statement lambda can contain any number of statements. Is this correct?**
True. However, a typical statement lambda does not exceed more than three lines. It is because using too many lines in a lambda expression may complicate the understanding, and in those cases, you should prefer a normal method over the lambda expression.

---

**POINTS TO REMEMBER**

At the time of this writing, you cannot use statement lambda for expression-bodied methods, but you can use expression lambda in those contexts. Apart from this, when you learn expression trees (an LINQ-related feature), you'll see that only expression lambdas can be used there, but you cannot use statement lambdas in those contexts. The discussion of expression trees is out of the scope of this book.

---

# Uses of Lambda Expressions

You can use lambda expressions in various scenarios. Let us examine some of them.

CHAPTER 3  LAMBDA EXPRESSIONS

# Event Subscription

The lambda expressions can be used to handle event notifications. To illustrate, let me add one more handler in Demonstration 3 of the previous chapter. However, this time, instead of creating a new method inside the Subscriber class (or creating a new subscriber class), let us handle the event notification using a lambda expression.

## Demonstration 3

Here is the complete program with the key changes in bold:

```
using static System.Console;

Publisher publisher = new();
// Attaching an event handler
publisher.ValueChanged += Subscriber.HandleFlagValueChanged;
// Creating a new variable and attaching it as an event handler
EventHandler<FlagChangedEventArgs> FlagChanged = ( sender, e) =>
{
    WriteLine($"The second handler: The flag value is changed to { e.Flag} ");
};
publisher.ValueChanged += FlagChanged;

publisher.Flag = 1;
publisher.Flag = 2;

// Detaching the event handlers
publisher.ValueChanged -= Subscriber.HandleFlagValueChanged;
publisher.ValueChanged -= FlagChanged;

publisher.Flag = 3;

// There is no change in the FlagChangedEventArgs,
// Publisher, and Subscriber classes. These are not
// shown to avoid repetition.
```

77

## CHAPTER 3  LAMBDA EXPRESSIONS

**Author's note:** You can download the *Ch3_Demo3_EventSubscriptionUsingLambda* project to execute the complete program on your computer.

## Output

Notice the changes in bold in the following output:

```
The flag value is changed to 1
The second handler: The flag value is changed to 1
The flag value is changed to 2
The second handler: The flag value is changed to 2
```

## Q&A Session

**Q3.7 Why did you use the FlagChanged variable? It appears to me that you could directly use the following code to handle the event notification:**

```
publisher.ValueChanged += (sender, e) =>
{
    WriteLine($"The second handler: The flag value is changed to {e.Flag} ");
};
```

Nice catch, but it was necessary. In the previous chapter (see the Useful Notes), you saw that I stored the anonymous method in a delegate variable so that I could unsubscribe it properly. The same issue is here as well. If you follow your proposed pattern, then you write the following code:

```
publisher.ValueChanged -= (sender,e) =>
{
    WriteLine($"Unsubscribing the event");
};
```

There is no guarantee that the event will be unsubscribed. *So, experts recommend that in such a case, you should store the anonymous method /lambda expression in an appropriate variable and then use it for subscribing to the event. As a result, you can keep track of it and unsubscribe whenever necessary.*

CHAPTER 3  LAMBDA EXPRESSIONS

**Author's note:** You can download the *Ch3_DiscussionOnDemo3* project to verify these code fragments on your computer.

> **POINT TO REMEMBER**
>
> To avoid memory leaks in real-world applications, once you subscribe to an event, you should unsubscribe from the same after the intended job is completed.

## Replacing the Anonymous Method

A lambda expression can replace an anonymous method. For example, the following program

```
using static System.Console;

int a = 12, b = 3;
Func<int, int, int> process = delegate (int x, int y) { return x + y; };
int result = process(12, 3);
WriteLine($"{a} + {b} is {result}");
```

can execute successfully and print:

```
12 + 3 is 15
```

If you replace the anonymous method with the lambda expression as follows:

```
Func<int, int, int> process = (x, y) => x + y;
```

You'll get the same output.

**Author's note:** You can download the *Ch3_UseOfLambdas* project to verify the code fragments presented in this section and the next two, where I'll cover the use of lambdas in parallel programming and functional programming.

CHAPTER 3  LAMBDA EXPRESSIONS

# Parallel Programming

The use of lambda expressions is seen in parallel programming. Here is a sample program that executes two tasks in parallel:

```
Task task1 = Task.Run(
    () =>
    {
        WriteLine("Task-1 starts executing...");
        for (int i = 0; i < 5; i++)
        {
            WriteLine(i);
            // Introducing some delay
            Thread.Sleep(2);
        }
        WriteLine("Task-1 is completed.");
    }
);

Task task2 = Task.Run(
    () =>
    {
        WriteLine("Task-2 starts executing...");
        // Mimic some delay
        Thread.Sleep(10);
        WriteLine("Task-2 is completed.");
    }
);
Task.WaitAll(task1, task2);
```

Here is a sample output from my computer (the output may vary in your system):

```
Task-2 starts executing...
Task-1 starts executing...
0
1
```

```
Task-2 is completed.
2
3
4
Task-1 is completed.
```

## Functional Programming

The use of lambda expressions is seen in functional programming as well. The online link Concepts and terminology (functional transformation) - LINQ to XML - .NET | Microsoft Learn[2] states

> *Historically, general-purpose functional programming languages, such as ML, Scheme, Haskell, and F#, have been primarily of interest to the academic community. Although it has always been possible to write pure functional transformations in C# and Visual Basic, the difficulty of doing so has not made it an attractive option to most programmers. In recent versions of these languages, however, new language constructs such as lambda expressions and type inference make functional programming much easier and more productive.*

The previous quote is self-explanatory. Let me add a few points to help you understand it better.

The functions are first-class citizens in FP. What does this mean? It indicates that you can use them like any other type. For example, you can assign a function to a variable, pass it as an argument to another function, or use it as a return type. It is possible to store them in data structures too.

In C#, delegate types can represent functions. So, **you can use lambda expressions to treat functions as first-class citizens**.

---

[2] https://learn.microsoft.com/en-us/dotnet/standard/linq/concepts-terminology-functional-transformation

CHAPTER 3    LAMBDA EXPRESSIONS

**Lambda is commonly used in LINQ queries, and the declarative nature of LINQ promotes functional programming (FP) as well.** Let me give you an example. Consider a list of numbers:

```
List<int> numbers= [10,25,102,62,97,505,233];
```

Now you can use LINQ method syntax (aka fluent syntax) to retrieve the numbers that are above 100 as follows:

```
numbers
  .Where(x => x > 100)
  .ToList()
  .ForEach((WriteLine));
```

If you investigate the Where function in the previous code segment, you'll see the following:

```
public static IEnumerable<TSource> Where<TSource>(this
  IEnumerable<TSource> source, Func<TSource, bool> predicate);
```

You can see that the Where function takes a Func<TSource, bool> as a parameter. It means it is a **higher-order function**. Creating or recognizing a higher-order function is another common activity in functional programming. The previous code segment shows that **you can pass a lambda inside a higher-order function** to exercise functional programming in C#.

## Q&A Session

### Q3.8 What is a higher-order function?
A higher-order function is a function with any of the following characteristics:

- It takes one or more functions as input
- It returns a function as output
- It can do both

CHAPTER 3  LAMBDA EXPRESSIONS

# Useful Notes

It'll be helpful for you to keep the following points in mind.

## Multiple Usages of the Token =>

You have seen me using the => as a **lambda operator**. You can also use this token in the **expression body definition** that has the following syntax:

```
member => expression;
```

To illustrate, consider a sample local function:

```
string Average(double x,double y)
{
    double temp = (x + y) / 2;
    return temp.ToString();
}
```

Using the expression-body method (C#6.0 onwards) syntax, you can write an equivalent code as follows:

```
string Average1(double x, double y) => ((x + y) / 2).ToString();
```

You may note that an expression-bodied method contains a single expression only. So, if you write something like the following:

```
// You cannot use a statement lambda like the following:
string Average2(double x, double y) =>
{
    double temp = (x + y) / 2;
    return temp.ToString();
};
```

You'll see compile-time errors.

**Author's note:** Download the *Ch3_UsingExpressionBodiedMethod* project to verify these code fragments.

83

CHAPTER 3   LAMBDA EXPRESSIONS

---
**POINTS TO REMEMBER**

---

The expression syntax to define non-lambda methods is not applicable to *statement lambdas*. You can use it only for expression *lambdas*.

---

# How Does the C# Compiler Transform the Lambdas?

Let's analyze the IL code of Demonstration 1 in this chapter. Here is a partial snapshot where you can see the C# code (that I wrote) and its decompiled version (also in C#):

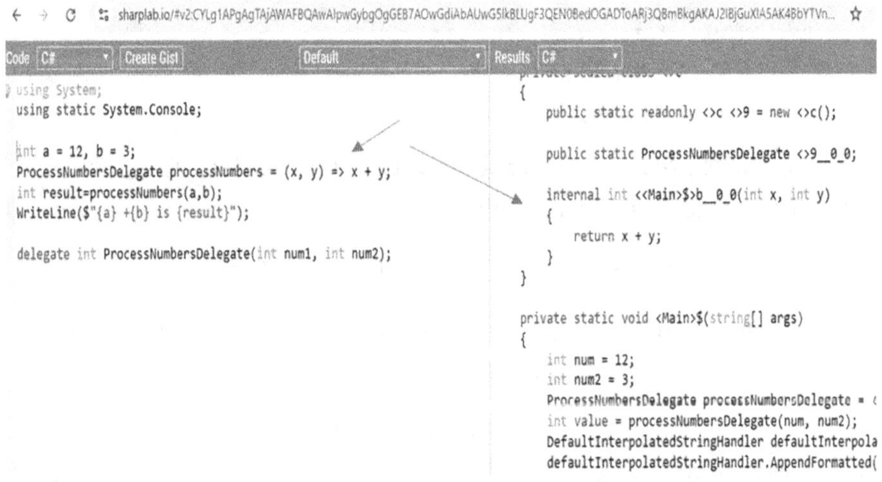

*Figure 3-1. Analyzing the IL code of Demonstration 1*

Figure 3-1 shows (follow the arrow tips) that the lambda expression: (x, y) => x + y; was decompiled into a method that takes two int parameters and returns the sum (which is an int as well) as follows:

CHAPTER 3　LAMBDA EXPRESSIONS

```
internal int <<Main>$>b__0_0(int x, int y)
{
   return x + y;
}
```

If you use similar lambda expressions, you'll see that **the C# compiler most of the time (but not always) converts these lambda expressions into methods like this** (do not worry about the method name—since you have not given it a name, C# has full freedom to choose any name for that anonymous method).

However, you wrap the delegate as a type parameter as follows:

```
Expression<Func<int, int, int>> expr = (x, y) => x + y;
```

**The C# compiler will not perform a similar conversion. This time, the compiler will build an expression tree** that represents the lambda expression.

## Latest Feature

We all know that in any popular programming language, feature enhancement may come in the latest releases. Those enhancements simplify your coding experience. The same is true for lambda expressions as well.

**Author's note:** You can learn about the latest features of C# 14 from What's new in C# 14 | Microsoft Learn.[3]

To illustrate, let me bring back the code that I used in Q1.9 in Chapter 1:

```
using static System.Console;

TryParseInt tryParseInt = IsValidInteger;
bool result = tryParseInt("10", out int number);
WriteLine($"Was the conversion successful? {result}");
WriteLine($"The number is {num}");
```

---

[3] https://learn.microsoft.com/en-us/dotnet/csharp/whats-new/csharp-14#simple-lambda-parameters-with-modifiers

CHAPTER 3  LAMBDA EXPRESSIONS

```
bool IsValidInteger(string inputString, out int number)
{
    bool flag = int.TryParse(inputString, out number);
    if (flag)
    {
        WriteLine($"Converted '{inputString}' to {number}.");
    }
    else
    {
        WriteLine($"Not a valid number.");
    }
    return flag;
}
delegate bool TryParseInt(string value1, out int value2);
```

Now you know lambda expressions. So, you can refactor this code as follows (notice the key change in bold):

```
using static System.Console;

int number;
TryParseInt tryParseInt = (string inputString, out int number) =>
{
    bool flag = int.TryParse(inputString, out number);
    if (flag)
    {
        WriteLine($"Converted '{inputString}' to {number}.");
    }
    else
    {
        WriteLine($"Not a valid number.");
    }
    return flag;
};

bool result = tryParseInt("10", out int num);
WriteLine($"Was the conversion successful? {result}");
WriteLine($"The number is {num}");
delegate bool TryParseInt(string value1, out int value2);
```

C#14 now allows **simple lambda parameters with modifiers**. This allows you to write the following as well (notice that I have used the out keyword as a parameter modifier, but I have not specified the parameter type of number):

```
using static System.Console;

TryParseInt tryParseInt = (inputString, out number) =>
{
    // There is no change in the remaining code that you saw in
    // the previous segment
```

If you are still using C#13, the previous code will not compile, and you'll see the following error:

```
CS8652 The feature 'simple lambda parameter modifiers' is currently in Preview
    and *unsupported*. To use Preview features, use the 'preview' language version.
```

**Author's note:** Download the *Ch3_TestingC#14Features* project to verify the program segments.

Cool features are indeed very tempting to use. However, you should not compromise the readability and understandability of the code while using those features.

## Further Reading

I hope that you have got a fair idea about lambda expressions in C#. As you work more on them, you may find some syntax limitations/restrictions. If needed, you can always read those from the official documentation Lambda expression warnings - C# reference | Microsoft Learn.[4]

---

[4] https://learn.microsoft.com/en-us/dotnet/csharp/language-reference/compiler-messages/lambda-expression-errors

CHAPTER 3  LAMBDA EXPRESSIONS

# Summary

This chapter discussed the following:

- What is a lambda expression? How does it help?
- What are the different types of lambda expressions in C#?
- What are some common uses of lambda expressions?
- What are the different uses of the => token?
- How does the C# compiler treat lambda expressions?

and many more...

# Exercise 3

Let's solve the following exercises.

| REMINDER |
|---|
| For all exercises in this book, you can assume that the following line: **using static System.Console;** has already been added at the top of each code segment. |

### E3.1 Can you predict the output of the following code?

```
var greet = x => WriteLine($"Hello {x}! How are you?");
greet("Joe");
```

### E3.2 Can you predict the output of the following code?

```
var a = "22";
var b = "28";
double c = 2.5;
```

```
Func<string, string, double, string> calculate = (x, y, z) =>
{
    var temp1 = int.Parse(x) + int.Parse(y);
    var temp2 = temp1 * z;
    return temp2.ToString();
};
var result = calculate(a, b, c);
WriteLine($"The calculated value is {result}");
```

**E3.3 Can you write an equivalent program of E3.2 using a custom delegate and an anonymous method?**

**E3.4 Can you predict the output of the following code?**

```
Func<(string, int), string> show = ((details) => $"{details.Item1} is now {details.Item2} years old.");
string result=show(("Kate", 25));
WriteLine(result);
```

**E3.5 In Ex2.5 of the previous chapter, you were supposed to work with a banking application. This application tags someone as an elite customer if the customer has at least $500. While implementing the solution, you saw me registering and unregistering an event without using lambda expressions. Now you know lambda expressions. Can you rewrite the solution using lambda expressions?**

# Keys to Exercise 3

Here is a sample solution set for the exercises in this chapter.

## E3.1

The code will not compile. You'll see the following error:

```
CS8917 The delegate type could not be inferred.
```

# CHAPTER 3 LAMBDA EXPRESSIONS

To fix this error, you can replace **the first line** of the given code segment with the following line of code:

```
var greet = (string x) => WriteLine($"Hello {x}! How are you?");
```

Or, you can use the following line as well:

```
Action<string> greet = x => WriteLine($"Hello {x}! How are you?");   // OK
```

Upon fixing the code, if you execute the program, you'll see the following output:

```
Hello Joe! How are you?
```

## E3.2

Here is the output:

```
The calculated value is 125
```

**Hint:** (22 + 28) * 2.5 =125

## E3.3

Here is an alternative program:

```
using static System.Console;

var a = "22";
var b = "28";
double c = 2.5;
CalculateDelegate calculate = delegate (string x, string y, double z)
{
    var temp1 = int.Parse(x) + int.Parse(y);
    var temp2 = temp1 * z;
    return temp2.ToString();
};
var result = calculate(a, b, c);
WriteLine($"The calculated value is: {result}");

delegate string CalculateDelegate(string x, string y, double z);
```

## E3.4

Here is the output:

```
Kate is now 25 years old.
```

**Author's note:** This program uses a tuple and a string as the delegate parameters. If you are not familiar with tuples, I suggest that you visit the online page Tuple types - C# reference | Microsoft Learn.

## E3.5

Here is a sample implementation in which there is no change in the BalanceChangedEventArgs and Bank classes. So, these two classes are not shown to avoid repetition. In addition, after introducing the lambda, the BalanceChecker class is no longer needed. I have kept the previous code in a comment so that you can compare the changes as well. Let's see the modified implementation:

```
using static System.Console;

Bank bank = new();
// bank.BalanceChanged += BalanceChecker.MarkElite;
EventHandler<BalanceChangedEventArgs> BalanceChanged= (sender, e) =>
    {
        WriteLine($"Current balance is {e.CurrentBalance}");
        if (e.CurrentBalance >= 500.0m)
        {
            Write($"Currently, you are an elite customer for us.\n");
        }
    };
bank.BalanceChanged +=BalanceChanged;

string input;
#region user input
try
{
    do
    {
```

## CHAPTER 3    LAMBDA EXPRESSIONS

```
            WriteLine("Enter amount (Type exit to quit application5):");
            input = ReadLine();
            if (input != "exit")
            {
                bank.UpdateBalance(decimal.Parse(input));
            }
        } while (input != "exit");
    }
    catch (Exception e)
    {
        WriteLine($"Error: {e}");
    }
    finally
    {
        // Detaching the event
        // bank.BalanceChanged -= BalanceChecker.MarkElite;
        bank.BalanceChanged -= BalanceChanged;
    }
    #endregion

    // The BalanceChecker class is no longer needed
    // class BalanceChecker
    // {
    //     public static void MarkElite(object? sender, BalanceChangedEventArgs e)
    //     {
    //         WriteLine($"Current balance is {e.CurrentBalance}");
    //         if (e.CurrentBalance >= 500.0m)
    //         {
    //             Write($"Currently, you are an elite customer for us.\n");
    //         }
    //     }
    // }

    // There is no change in the BalanceChangedEventArgs and Bank classes.
    // So, these are not shown to avoid repetitions
```

**Author's note:** You can download the **Ex3.5_BankingApp** project to execute the complete implementation.

92

# CHAPTER 4

# Bonus

After completing the book's first three chapters, I assume you have a fair idea about using delegates, events, and lambda expressions in C# programming. This chapter provides some supplementary material and investigates more on delegates and events. It also provides some in-depth discussions and alternative implementations for some of the demonstrations that you have seen earlier. Let's start.

## More on Delegates

When a delegate instance targets a method, the signature of the delegate type and the target method need not be an exact match. To understand the delegate's compatibility, it is essential to be aware of the underlying concept. While answering Q1.2 of Chapter 1, I talked about covariance and contravariance. Let's examine them in detail.

## Covariance

The official documentation Variance in Delegates - C# | Microsoft Learn[1] states

---

[1] https://learn.microsoft.com/en-us/dotnet/csharp/programming-guide/concepts/covariance-contravariance/variance-in-delegates

## CHAPTER 4  BONUS

> ... you can assign to delegates not only methods that have matching signatures, but also methods that return more derived types ...

This is covariance. You can see that it talks about **return type compatibility**. Let's examine covariance with a simple program.

In the upcoming demonstration, you'll see a Vehicle class that has a single method, GetVehicle, as follows:

```
class Vehicle
{
    public Vehicle GetVehicle()
    {
        WriteLine("Returning a vehicle.");
        return this;
    }
}
```

Since the return type of the GetVehicle method is Vehicle, the following assignment will not cause any problem:

```
Func<Vehicle> vehicleDelegate = vehicle.GetVehicle;
```

**Author's note**: In this line of code, vehicle is a Vehicle object.

Now, assume there is another class, called Bus, that derives from the Vehicle class. It has the following look:

```
class Bus:Vehicle
{
    public Bus GetBus()
    {
        WriteLine("Returning a bus.");
        return this;
    }
}
```

You can see that the return type of the GetBus method is Bus, but not Vehicle. However, since the Bus class is derived from the Vehicle class, covariance allows you the following assignment:

```
vehicleDelegate = bus.GetBus;
```

**Author's note:** In this line of code, bus is a Bus object.

## Demonstration 1

It's time to see a complete program that is as follows:

```
using static System.Console;

Vehicle vehicle = new();
Bus bus = new();

// Assigning a method with a matching signature
Func<Vehicle> vehicleDelegate = vehicle.GetVehicle;
_ = vehicleDelegate();

// Covariance allows the following assignment
vehicleDelegate = bus.GetBus;
_=vehicleDelegate();

// The vehicle class and the Bus class are placed here
// These are not shown to avoid repetitions.
```

**Author's note:** You can download the project Ch4_Demo1_Covariance to execute the complete program.

## Output

Upon executing this program, you'll see the following output:

```
Returning a vehicle.
Returning a bus.
```

CHAPTER 4   BONUS

**Author's note:** I have used the built-in Func delegate in this example. You can examine covariance using a custom delegate as well. I have kept the alternative code commented in the Ch2_Demo1_Covariance project that you can download from the Apress website.

## Q&A Session

### Q4.1 When I investigate Func<Vehicle> in Visual Studio, I see the following:

```
public delegate TResult Func<out TResult>() where TResult : allows ref struct;
```

**What is the role of the "out" parameter here?**

The out keyword can be used in two different contexts:

- It can be used as a parameter modifier.

- It can be used in generic type parameter declarations for interfaces and delegates. This case confirms that the type parameter is covariant.

Now you understand that in our example, the return type is covariant.

**Author's note:** The official link https://learn.microsoft.com/en-us/dotnet/csharp/language-reference/keywords/out summarizes the useful scenarios and restrictions of the out parameter.

## Contravariance

It is no wonder that you can assign to delegates those methods that have matching signatures. You have also learned that covariance allows you to assign methods that return more derived types. Now you'll learn about contravariance that allows you to assign methods that accept parameters of less derived types as well. Let's examine this.

In the upcoming example, you'll see two classes where the `ElectricCar` class derives from the `Car` class. The `Car` class has a method, `Describe` as follows:

```
public void Describe(Car car)
{
    WriteLine($"This {car} can run at 100 mph.");
}
```

The `ElectricCar` class has a method, called `DisplayFeature` as follows:

```
public void DisplayFeature(ElectricCar ecar)
{
    WriteLine($"This is an {ecar}");
}
```

Since the return type of the `DisplayFeature` method is void, you can exercise the following assignment without any problem (`electricCar` is an `ElectricCar` instance)

```
Action<ElectricCar> vehicleDelegate = electricCar.DisplayFeature;
```

However, can you assign the `Describe` method (of the `Car` class) to `vehicleDelegate`? **The answer is yes.** Though the Describe method accepts a `Car` parameter that is less derived than `ElectricCar`, contravariance allows this assignment. So, you'll find no issue with the following assignment (car is a `Car` instance):

```
vehicleDelegate = car.Describe; // OK
```

## Demonstration 2

Let's see a complete program that is as follows:

```
using static System.Console;

Car car = new();
ElectricCar electricCar = new();
```

```csharp
// Assigning a method with a matching signature
Action<ElectricCar> vehicleDelegate = electricCar.DisplayFeature;
vehicleDelegate(electricCar);

// Contravariance allows the following assignment
vehicleDelegate = car.Describe; // OK
class Car
{
    public void Describe(Car car)
    {
        WriteLine($"This {car} can run at 100 mph.");
    }
    public override string ToString()
    {
        return "car";
    }
}
class ElectricCar : Car
{
    public void DisplayFeature(ElectricCar ecar)
    {
        WriteLine($"This is an {ecar}");
    }
    public override string ToString()
    {
        return "electric car";
    }
}
```

## Output

Upon executing this program, you'll see the following output:

```
This is an electric car
This electric car can run at 100 mph.
```

CHAPTER 4  BONUS

## Analysis

Notice that in the following code:

```
// Contravariance allows the following assignment
vehicleDelegate = car.Describe; // OK
vehicleDelegate(electricCar);
```

the `Action<ElectricCar>` instance(`vehicleDelegate`) was expecting a method that accepts an `ElectricCar` instance. However, it was assigned the `Describe` method, which takes a more general `Car` type (in other words, the `Describe` method accepts a base type parameter). Why did the compiler allow this? It's safe. Since `Describe` can work with any `Car` instance, it will find no difficulties working with an `ElectricCar` instance.

You understand that car.Describe(Car car) matches Action<Car>. But we assigned it to an Action<ElectricCar>. However, this code compiles **because Action<T> is contravariant in T (in T).**

---
**POINTS TO NOTE**

---

If you carefully analyze covariance and contravariance in delegates, you'll understand that these points remind you of the ordinary polymorphic behavior. For example, while programming to an interface, you often invoke a method and get back a type that is more specific than what you expected. It is also common that while invoking a method, you can supply argument(s) that have more specific types than the parameter(s) of the method. So, it is no wonder that delegates support the concept.

## Q&A Session

### Q4.2 When I investigate the Action<ElectricCar> in Visual Studio, I see the following:

```
public delegate void Action<in T>(T obj) where T : allows ref struct;
```

99

### What is the role of the "in" parameter here?

The in keyword can be used in many different contexts (such as a parameter modifier, inside a foreach statement, inside the LINQ queries, and as generic type parameters in generic delegates and interfaces). However, in this example, the in keyword is used to indicate that the parameter type is contravariant.

**Author's note:** The official link https://learn.microsoft.com/en-us/dotnet/csharp/language-reference/keywords/in summarizes the use of the in parameter.

### Q4.3 While examining covariance and contravariance, in both demonstrations, you have used built-in Func and Action delegates. Was this intentional?

Using built-in delegates, I could avoid declaring the custom delegates and shorten my code.

### Q4.4 Will I see the same result if I replace them with custom delegates?

Yes, using the custom delegates, you'll see the same output. I have kept those alternative codes in comments. If you download the projects—**Ch4_Demo1_Covariance** and **Ch2_Demo2_Contravariance**, you can see the alternative implementations as well.

---

**POINT TO REMEMBER**

C# provides variance support for reference types, but not for value types. This is why you'll see implicit conversions between generic types, delegates, and arrays are possible when the type parameters are reference types.

# More on Events

You have learned event handling in Chapter 2. In Chapter 3, you also subscribed to an event using lambda expressions. Now you'll learn something more about them.

## Event Accessors

In Chapter 2, you have seen me declaring the event in every demonstration. Arbitrarily, let's consider Demonstration 2 of Chapter 2, where I declared the event in the Publisher class as follows:

```
public event ValueChangedEventHandler? ValueChanged;
```

To investigate this line in detail, let's see the IL code (notice the key portions shown in bold).

**Author's note:** To show you the IL code, I have used the online tool SharpLab (https://sharplab.io/).

```
// Some code
internal class Publisher
{
    private int flag;

    [CompilerGenerated]
    private ValueChangedEventHandler m_ValueChanged;
    // Some other code
    public event ValueChangedEventHandler ValueChanged
    {
        [CompilerGenerated]
        add
        {
            ValueChangedEventHandler valueChangedEventHandler = this.ValueChanged;
```

## CHAPTER 4  BONUS

```
            while (true)
            {
                ValueChangedEventHandler valueChangedEventHandler2 =
                   valueChangedEventHandler;
                ValueChangedEventHandler value2 = (ValueChangedEventHandler)
                   Delegate.Combine(valueChangedEventHandler2, value);
                valueChangedEventHandler = Interlocked.CompareExchange(ref
                   this.ValueChanged, value2, valueChangedEventHandler2);
                if ((object)valueChangedEventHandler == valueChangedEventHandler2)
                {
                    break;
                }
            }
        }
        [CompilerGenerated]
        remove
        {
            ValueChangedEventHandler valueChangedEventHandler = this.ValueChanged;
            while (true)
            {
                ValueChangedEventHandler valueChangedEventHandler2 =
                   valueChangedEventHandler;
                ValueChangedEventHandler value2 = (ValueChangedEventHandler)
                   Delegate.Remove(valueChangedEventHandler2, value);
                valueChangedEventHandler = Interlocked.CompareExchange(ref
                   this.ValueChanged, value2, valueChangedEventHandler2);
                if ((object)valueChangedEventHandler == valueChangedEventHandler2)
                {
                    break;
                }
            }
        }
// Some other code
```

This IL code shows that when you write:

```
public event ValueChangedEventHandler? ValueChanged;
```

The following things happen:

- The compiler creates a private delegate field and a public pair of event accessors, named add and remove.

- It ensures that you work on a multicast delegate (see the presence of the Combine and Remove methods).

- The compiler ensures the thread safety (see the use of the Interlocked class).

---
**POINT TO NOTE**

---

You use the get and set accessors while using the properties. Now you can see that the add and remove accessors are used when you use events.

---

After knowing this info, you can write an alternative implementation for Demonstration 2 of Chapter 2 by explicitly implementing the event accessors and locking mechanism. Let's see this alternative code in the following demonstration.

## Demonstration 3

Here is the alternative program for Demonstration 2 of Chapter 2 with the key changes in bold (I have kept the old code in comments):

```
using static System.Console;

Publisher publisher = new();
// Attaching an event handler
publisher.ValueChanged += Subscriber.HandleFlagValueChanged;
publisher.Flag = 1;
```

103

CHAPTER 4    BONUS

```
publisher.Flag = 2;
// Detaching the event handler
publisher.ValueChanged -= Subscriber.HandleFlagValueChanged;
publisher.Flag = 3;

delegate void ValueChangedEventHandler(object? sender,
    FlagChangedEventArgs e);

class FlagChangedEventArgs : EventArgs
{
    public int Flag { get; }
    public FlagChangedEventArgs(int flag)
    {
        Flag = flag;
    }
}
class Publisher
{
    int flag = 0;

    // Declare the event

    // The following line was used in Demonstration 2 of Chapter 2
    // public event ValueChangedEventHandler? ValueChanged;

    #region alternative code using explicit accessors
    private readonly object _lockObject = new();
    private event ValueChangedEventHandler? _valueChanged;
    public event ValueChangedEventHandler? ValueChanged
    {
        add
        {
            lock (_lockObject)
            {
                _valueChanged += value;
            }
        }
```

```csharp
            remove
            {
                lock (_lockObject)
                {
                    _valueChanged -= value;
                }
            }
        }
        #endregion

        public int Flag
        {
            get { return flag; }
            set
            {
                flag = value;
                OnValueChanged(new FlagChangedEventArgs(flag));
            }
        }
        protected virtual void OnValueChanged(FlagChangedEventArgs e)
        {
            // if (ValueChanged != null)
            // {
            //     ValueChanged(this, e);
            // }
            // Simplified form:
            // ValueChanged?.Invoke(this, e);
            _valueChanged?.Invoke(this, e);
        }
    }
    class Subscriber
    {
        internal static void HandleFlagValueChanged(object? sender,
          FlagChangedEventArgs e)
```

CHAPTER 4  BONUS

```
    {
        WriteLine($"The flag value in {sender} is changed to {e.Flag}");
    }
}
```

## Output

Once again, you'll see the following output when you run this program:

```
The flag value in Publisher is changed to 1
The flag value in Publisher is changed to 2
```

## Q&A Session

**Q4.5 What are the key benefits of using user-defined event accessors?**
There are some typical corner cases, such as while providing a custom behavior or implementing an explicit interface event, you'll find its usefulness. A typical case study on this is analyzed in Demonstration 4 of this chapter.

## Interface Events

An interface can declare events. Let me show you an example. I showed you an alternative program for Demonstration 2 of Chapter 2 in the previous demonstration. This time, let me modify Demonstration 3 of Chapter 2 and show you the changes only (in bold):

```
// There is no change in the previous section of the program

interface IPublisher
{
    event EventHandler<FlagChangedEventArgs>? ValueChanged;
}
class Publisher:IPublisher
{
    int flag = 0;
```

```
    // Declare the event
    public event EventHandler<FlagChangedEventArgs>? ValueChanged;

// There is no change in the remaining part of the program
```

Once you run this modified program, you'll see the same output:

```
The flag value in Publisher is changed to 1
The flag value in Publisher is changed to 2
```

**Author's note:** You can download the project **Ch4_InterfaceEvents** to execute the complete program.

**Sometimes your class can inherit from multiple interfaces. In a typical case, each interface can contain an event with the same name. In this case, you can explicitly implement the interfaces.** However, while writing an explicit interface implementation for the event, you must provide implementations for the add and remove accessors. Let's see the following demonstration.

**Author's note:** Since the compiler usually provides the add and remove accessors automatically, you don't need to define them yourself. However, if you do, the compiler will not generate them.

## Demonstration 4

This program has the following characteristics:

- There are two interfaces, named IBefore and IAfter. Each interface declares an event named ValueChanged.

- The two events need to be raised at different times. One should be raised before changing a value (named, flag), and another event should be raised after changing the value inside the Publisher class.

- The Publisher class implements both the IBefore and IAfter interfaces.

CHAPTER 4   BONUS

- As said before, in this case, you need to provide an explicit interface implementation **for at least one of the events**. So, arbitrarily, I have decided to explicitly implement the IBefore interface.
- There are two methods in the Subscriber class to handle these events.

Let's see the sample implementation now.

```
using System.Text;
using static System.Console;

Publisher publisher = new();

IBefore before = publisher;
IAfter after = publisher;

// Attaching the event handlers
before.ValueChanged += Subscriber.HandleFlagValueChangedBefore;
after.ValueChanged += Subscriber.HandleFlagValueChangedAfter;

publisher.Flag = 1;
publisher.Flag = 2;

// Detaching the event handlers
before.ValueChanged -= Subscriber.HandleFlagValueChangedBefore;
after.ValueChanged -= Subscriber.HandleFlagValueChangedAfter;
publisher.Flag = 3;

// Using the primary constructor feature (C#12 onward)
class FlagChangedEventArgs(int flag) : EventArgs
{
    public int Flag { get; } = flag;
}

interface IBefore
{
    event EventHandler<FlagChangedEventArgs>? ValueChanged;
}
```

```
interface IAfter
{
    event EventHandler<FlagChangedEventArgs>? ValueChanged;
}
class Publisher : IBefore, IAfter
{
    int flag = 0;
    private readonly object _lockObject = new();

    // Need to work on each interface event
    // In this case, you need to provide an explicit interface
    // implementation for at least one of the events.
    // Arbitrarily, I have decided to do that for
    // the IBefore interface
    private event EventHandler<FlagChangedEventArgs>? _beforeValueChanged;
    public event EventHandler<FlagChangedEventArgs>? ValueChanged;

    event EventHandler<FlagChangedEventArgs>? IBefore.ValueChanged
    {
        add
        {
            lock (_lockObject)
            {
                _beforeValueChanged += value;
            }
        }
        remove
        {
            lock (_lockObject)
            {
                _beforeValueChanged -= value;
            }
        }
    }
```

CHAPTER 4  BONUS

```
    public int Flag
    {
        get { return flag; }
        set
        {
            OnBeforeValueChanged(new FlagChangedEventArgs(flag));
            flag = value;
            OnAfterValueChanged(new FlagChangedEventArgs(flag));
        }
    }
    protected virtual void OnBeforeValueChanged(FlagChangedEventArgs e)
    {
        _beforeValueChanged?.Invoke(this, e);
    }
    protected virtual void OnAfterValueChanged(FlagChangedEventArgs e)
    {
        ValueChanged?.Invoke(this, e);
    }
}
class Subscriber
{
    internal static void HandleFlagValueChangedBefore(object? sender,
        FlagChangedEventArgs e)
    {
        WriteLine($"The flag value in {sender} is about to be changed from
            {e.Flag}");
    }
    internal static void HandleFlagValueChangedAfter(object? sender,
        FlagChangedEventArgs e)
    {
        WriteLine($"The flag value in {sender} is changed to {e.Flag}");
    }
}
```

## Output

Upon executing the program, you should see the following output:

```
The flag value in Publisher is about to be changed from 0
The flag value in Publisher is changed to 1
The flag value in Publisher is about to be changed from 1
The flag value in Publisher is changed to 2
```

## Events in a GUI App

A graphical user interface (GUI) is easy to interact with. A GUI application can have graphical elements such as buttons, text boxes, menus, and labels (and many more items) to simplify the user's experience. These applications are highly event-driven.

There are many common frameworks for creating a GUI application, such as Windows Forms (WinForms), Windows Presentation Foundation (WPF), and Multi-platform App UI (MAUI). You may be familiar with one or more of them. Since a GUI application is highly event-driven, let's make a WinForms application and analyze the code.

## Demonstration 5

To simplify our discussion, let us assume our application will display a form with a single button, and when you click the button, a message box will appear with the text "Hello, reader!". If you are new to WinForms, here's a quick summary of the steps (if you're already familiar, feel free to skip this part):

- Create a new project using the "Windows Forms App" template. Give the name of the project, choose a storage location, and select the appropriate framework. For example, I named the project **Ch4_Demo5_**

CHAPTER 4  BONUS

**WinFormApp**, stored it in the same location where the other projects in this chapter were stored, and selected **.NET 10.0 (Preview)** while building this application.

- From the Toolbox, drag a button onto the form. Leave the control name as **button1**, but change its text property to **"Test."** For your quick reference, I have snipped out the mentioned settings from Visual Studio and shown them in the following figure (Figure 4-1):

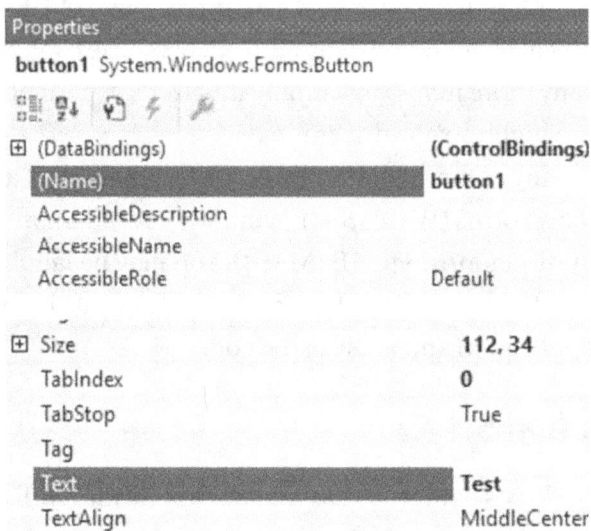

***Figure 4-1.*** *The Name and Text properties of the button added to the form*

CHAPTER 4　BONUS

- Now the form may look like the following (**see Figure 4-2**):

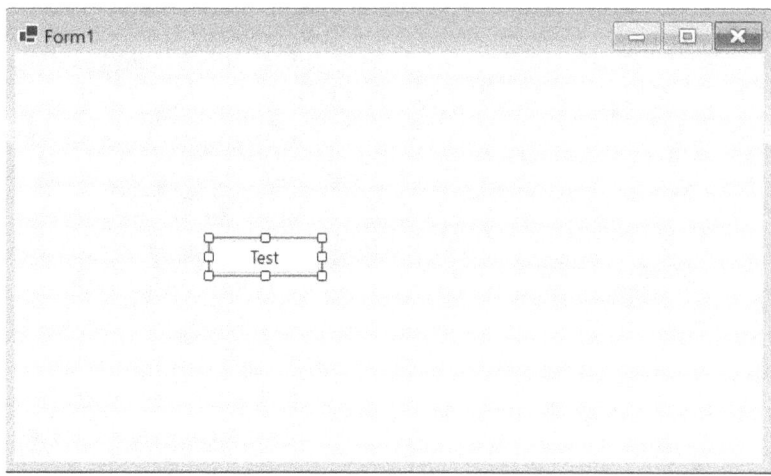

*Figure 4-2. Placing the "Test" button on Form1*

- Select this button, open the **Properties** window, and click the **Events** button. Name the Click event as TestBtnClickHandler (follow the arrow tips in the following figure). Now it may appear something like below (**see Figure 4-3**):

113

CHAPTER 4   BONUS

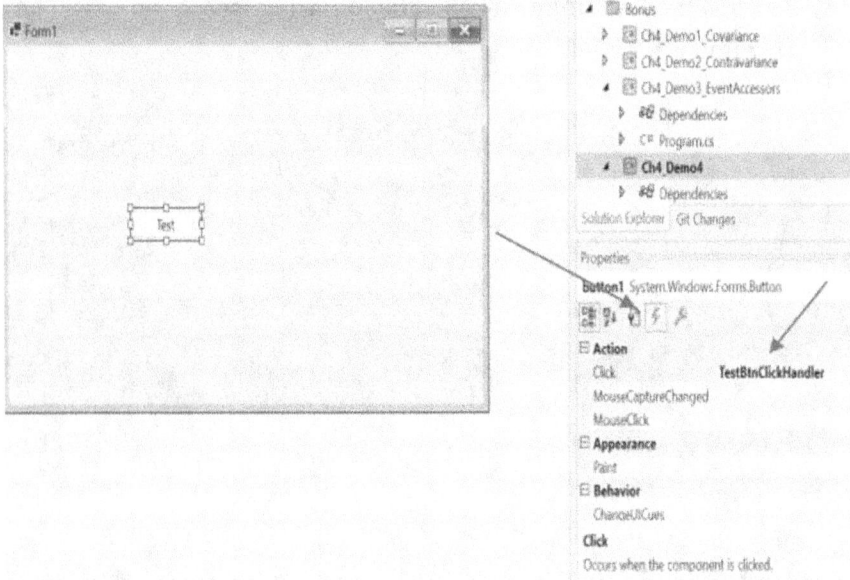

*Figure 4-3. Setting the Click event name as* `TestBtnClickHandler`

- Double-click the **'Test'** button, which will open the **Form1.cs** file, and you'll see the method template is ready for you. Let's write the following code (shown in bold) for the event handler.

  ```
  private void TestBtnClickHandler(object sender, EventArgs e)
  {
      MessageBox.Show("Hello, reader!");
  }
  ```

- Save the changes.

## Output

While running the application now, if you click on the **Test** button, you'll see the message: Hello, reader! in a message box as shown in **Figure 4-4**.

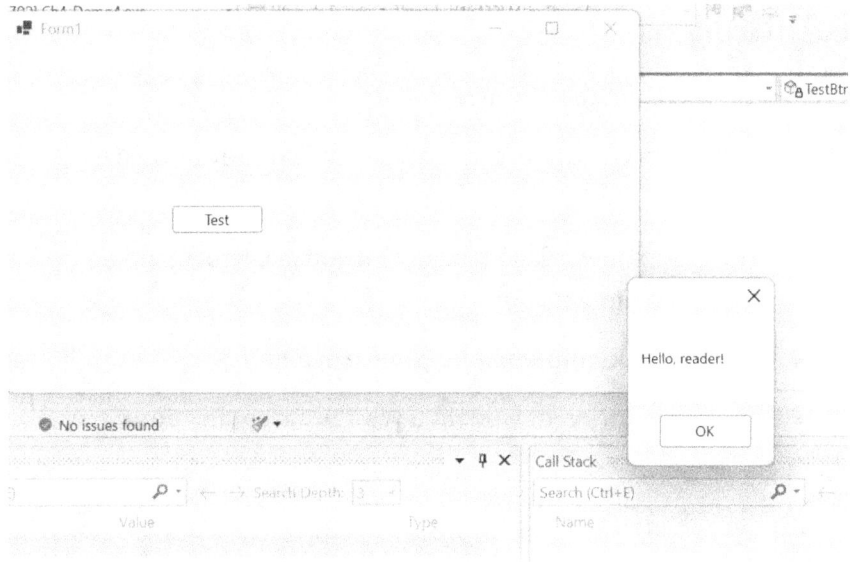

***Figure 4-4.*** *Output snapshot from Visual Studio when you click the Test button*

## Analysis

If you analyze the code, you'll see that the following event was declared:

```
public event EventHandler? Click;
```

and the event registration was completed:

```
button1.Click += TestBtnClickHandler;
```

You can see that the fundamental steps of event handling are also implemented in this GUI application.

This is the end of the book. Happy coding!

CHAPTER 4   BONUS

# Summary

This chapter discussed the following:

- How does C# support covariance and contravariance in delegates?
- How can you work with custom event accessors, and when are these useful?
- How can you implement interface events?
- How does an event work in a WinForms application?

and many more...

# Exercise 4

Let's solve the following exercises.

> **REMINDER**
>
> You can assume that the following line: `using static System.Console;` is added before each of the code segments.

**E4.1 Can you compile the following code?**

```
Func<int, int, object> add = Sum;
WriteLine(add(12, 13));
string Sum(int a, int b) => $"{a} + {b} = {a+b}";
```

**E4.2 Can you compile the following code?**

```
Func<string, string> display = PrintInfo;
WriteLine(display("Hi"));
string PrintInfo(object o)
```

```
{
    return $"'{o}' is of type: {o.GetType().Name}";
}
```

### E4.3 Can you compile the following code?

```
Func<int,string> display = PrintInfo;
// Some other code, if any
string PrintInfo(object o)
{
    return $"'{o}' is of type: {o.GetType().Name}";
}
```

### E4.4 Can you compile the following code?

```
using static System.Console;

Func<string, string> display = PrintInfo1;
display += PrintInfo2;
WriteLine(display("hello"));
string PrintInfo1(string s)
{
    return "This is a beautiful day";
}
string PrintInfo2(object o)
{
    return $"{o} is of type: {o.GetType().Name}";
}
```

**E4.5** Often, while executing a long-running method, we'd like to monitor its progress. Can you implement such an application? Of course, you can! To build it, you can use both delegates and events. Since you've now completed this book, I'd like you to implement the idea using **delegates** for reporting progress and **events** for signaling completion. When the execution finishes, the application should congratulate the caller by invoking an event. Give it a try!

Here is an output from my sample implementation that you'll see at the end of the chapter:

```
20% of the work is done.
40% of the work is done.
60% of the work is done.
80% of the work is done.
100% of the work is done.
Congratulations on your success! You have completed 100% of the work.
```

**Author's note:** I report progress after the completion of at least 20%. It's a choice. If you want, you can vary the percentage slab.

## Keys to Exercise 4

Here is a sample solution set for the exercises in this chapter.

## E4.1

Yes. In this code, the Sum method returns a string, but the delegate expects an object. However, the string class implicitly inherits from the System.Object class, and you know that object type is an alias for System.Object in .NET. So, due to the covariance support in C#, there was no problem with the following assignment:

```
Func<int, int, object> add = Sum;
```

As a result, upon executing the code, you'll see the following output:

```
12 + 13 = 25
```

## E4.2

Yes. In this code, the PrintInfo method accepts an object as a parameter, but the Func<string, string> instance expects a method that has a string parameter. However, you know that the string class implicitly inherits from the `object` class. So, due to the contravariance support in C#, there was no problem with the following assignment:

```
Func<string, string> display = PrintInfo;
```

As a result, upon executing the code, you'll see the following output:

```
'Hi' is of type: String
```

## E4.3

No. In this code, the `PrintInfo` method accepts an `object` as a parameter, but the `Func<int, string>` instance expects a method that has an `int` parameter. **Though the int class implicitly inherits from the object class, you do not see the contravariance support in this example. It is because int is a value type but not a reference type.** So, the following assignment:

```
Func<int, string> display = PrintInfo;
```

Will raise the compile-time error saying:

```
CS0123   No overload for 'PrintInfo(object)' matches delegate 'Func<int, string>'
```

## E4.4

This program will produce the following output:

```
hello is of type: String
```

This example exercises multicasting. However, notice that the target methods have a non-void return type. This is why, in this multicast delegate invocation, you see the return value from the last method in the invocation list. Though other methods are also called, those values are discarded in between.

CHAPTER 4  BONUS

# E4.5

Here is a sample implementation:

```
using static System.Console;

Publisher publisher = new();
EventHandler<PercentageCompleteEventArgs> ProgressStatus = (sender, e) =>
{
    WriteLine($"Congratulations on your success! You have completed
       {e.CompletePercentage}% of the work.");
};
publisher.ProgressChanged += ProgressStatus;
try
{
    Action<int> progress = DisplayProgress;
    publisher.PerformLengthyWork(progress);
    static void DisplayProgress(int completePercentage)
    {
        WriteLine($"{completePercentage}% of the work is done.");
    }
}
catch (Exception e)
{
    WriteLine($"Error: {e}");
}
finally
{
    // Detaching the event
    publisher.ProgressChanged -= ProgressStatus;
}
class PercentageCompleteEventArgs : EventArgs
{
    public int CompletePercentage { get; }
    public PercentageCompleteEventArgs(int completePercentage)
    {
```

```
        CompletePercentage = completePercentage;
    }
}
class Publisher
{
    public event EventHandler<PercentageCompleteEventArgs>? ProgressChanged;
    public void PerformLengthyWork(Action<int> doWork)
    {
        for (int i = 1; i <= 5; i++)
        {
            // Mimicking the lengthy work
            Thread.Sleep(100);
            int percentage = i * 20;
            // Invoking the delegate
            doWork(percentage);
            // You can raise the event to display the progress as well
            // OnProgressChanged(new PercentageCompleteEventArgs
            // (percentage));
            if (i == 5)
            {
                // The job is completed. Raising the event.
                OnProgressChanged(new PercentageCompleteEventArgs(percentage));
            }
        }
    }
    protected virtual void OnProgressChanged(PercentageCompleteEventArgs e)
    {
        ProgressChanged?.Invoke(this, e);
    }
}
```

# APPENDIX A

# What's Next?

You've now explored delegates, events, and lambda expressions—powerful tools at the heart of advanced C# programming. These concepts aren't just features; they're stepping stones to writing cleaner, smarter, and more flexible code. However, we all know that mastery doesn't come from reading alone—it comes from **doing**. Keep experimenting. Build small projects. Break things and fix them. Each line of code you write will sharpen your skills and deepen your understanding. In my own journey, I've learned that growth comes from a cycle of curiosity, practice, and learning from others. I revisit the official documentation (`https://learn.microsoft.com/en-us/dotnet/csharp/`), read widely from different authors, follow online courses, and learn from the community discussions. You can do the same—and perhaps even more. The road to becoming an exceptional developer never truly ends, but every step you take makes you stronger. Keep walking it with patience, persistence, and passion.

## Recommended Books

The following titles cover a broad range of C# topics and will help you continue building your skills:

- *C# 12 in a Nutshell* by Joseph Albahari (O'Reilly Media, 1st edition, December 2023)

- *Professional C#* by Christian Nagel (Wrox, 8th Edition, August 2021)

- *The C# Player's Guide* by RB Whitaker (Starbound Software, 5th Edition, January 2022)
- *C# 13 and .NET 9 – Modern Cross-Platform Development Fundamentals* by Mark J. Price (Packt Publishing, November 2024)
- *C# 4.0 The Complete Reference* by Herbert Schildt (McGraw Hill, May 2010)

**Author's note:** The last book in my list may be outdated, but it offers unique insights and code explanations that are still worth your time. This is why I have kept it in my list of recommended books.

## Other Resources

While there is no shortage of online articles today, it's important to validate the information before relying on it. I strongly encourage you to consult the official Microsoft documentation (mentioned earlier) whenever you need to clarify a concept or resolve a doubt. It is always your most reliable source of information.

You'll also find many online courses that can help you strengthen your understanding. Choose what fits your style. As a starting point, I recommend this LinkedIn Learning course, which provides a clear and concise introduction to delegates, events, and lambda expressions: C# Delegates, Events, and Lambdas – LinkedIn Learning.[1]

---

[1] https://www.linkedin.com/learning/c-sharp-delegates-events-and-lambdas-14503458

# APPENDIX B

# Author's Other Books

The following list includes other Apress books by the author:

- *Python Bootcamp* (Apress, 2025)
- *Creational Design Patterns in Java* (Apress, Upcoming)
- *Creational Design Patterns in C#* (Apress, 2025)
- *Task Programming in C# and .NET* (Apress, 2025)
- *Parallel Programming with C# and .NET* (Apress, 2024)
- *Introducing Functional Programming Using C#* (Apress, 2023)
- *Simple and Efficient Programming in C# Second Edition* (Apress, 2022)
- *Test Your Skills in C# Programming* (Apress, 2022)
- *Java Design Patterns Third Edition* (Apress, 2022)
- *Simple and Efficient Programming in C#* (Apress, 2021)
- *Design Patterns in C# Second Edition* (Apress, 2020)
- *Getting Started with Advanced C#* (Apress, 2020)
- *Interactive Object-Oriented Programming in Java Second Edition* (Apress, 2019)
- *Java Design Patterns Second Edition* (Apress, 2019)

## APPENDIX B   AUTHOR'S OTHER BOOKS

- *Design Patterns in C#* (Apress, 2018)
- *Interactive C#* (Apress, 2017)
- *Interactive Object-Oriented Programming in Java* (Apress, 2016)
- *Java Design Patterns* (Apress, 2016)

**The following list includes his non-Apress books:**

- *Python Bookcamp* (Amazon, 2021)
- *Operating System: Computer Science Interview Series* (Createspace, 2014)

To learn more about these books, you can refer to any of the following links:

- https://amazon.com/author/vaskaran_sarcar
- https://link.springer.com/search?newsearch=true&query=vaskaran+sarcar&content-type=book&dateFrom=&dateTo=&sortBy=newestFirst

GPSR Compliance

The European Union's (EU) General Product Safety Regulation (GPSR) is a set of rules that requires consumer products to be safe and our obligations to ensure this.

If you have any concerns about our products, you can contact us on

ProductSafety@springernature.com

In case Publisher is established outside the EU, the EU authorized representative is:

Springer Nature Customer Service Center GmbH
Europaplatz 3
69115 Heidelberg, Germany

www.ingramcontent.com/pod-product-compliance
Lightning Source LLC
LaVergne TN
LVHW020413070526
838199LV00054B/3596